RS
...kbook

All the questions on all the topics, immaculately presented and dangerously close to being funny.

Contents

Section One — Perspectives

Spirituality 1
The Nature of Truth 2
Believing in God 3
Religious Experiences 4
The Nature of God 5
Christian and Jewish Teaching on God 6
Muslim Teaching on God 7
Evil and Suffering 8
Judaism and Islam — Evil & Suffering 9
The Origin of the World 10
Life After Death 11
Jewish Beliefs about Life After Death 12
Muslim Beliefs about Life After Death 13
Life & Death and the Christian View 14
Life & Death in Judaism 15
Life & Death in Islam 16
Fertility Treatment 17
Marriage in Christianity 18
The Christian Church and Divorce 19
Marriage in Judaism 20
Marriage in Islam 21
Religious Attitudes to Sex 22
Children and Religion 23
Prejudice and Equality 24
Race and Religion 25
Injustice and Protest 26
Jewish Attitudes towards Equality 27
Muslim Attitudes towards Equality 28
Christianity and Other Religions 29
Judaism, Islam and Other Religions 30
Christianity and Poverty 31
Judaism, Islam and Poverty 32
Religion and the Environment 33
Religion and Animals 34
Religion and Crime 35
Christianity and War 36
Judaism, Islam and War 37
Religion and Drugs 38
Religion and the Media 39

Section Two — Christianity

Basic Christian Beliefs 40
The Bible 41
Christian Values 42
Love and Forgiveness 43
The Sermon on the Mount 44
Spreading the Gospel 45
Living the Christian Life 46
The Church 47
Traditions and Denominations 48
Members of the Church 49
A Christian Church 50
Religious Symbolism 51
Sunday Worship 52
Christian Festivals 53
Private Prayer and the Sacraments 54
Baptism 55
Funerals, Burial and Cremation 56
Jesus and Mark's Gospel 57
The Kingdom of God 58
Jesus and Miracles 59
Miracles, Faith and Conflict 60
Discipleship 61
Jesus' Trial and Death 62

Section Three — Judaism

The Beginnings of Judaism 63
Basic Jewish Beliefs 64
Sources of Guidance 65
The Holocaust 66
Different Jewish Traditions 67
Judaism and Day-to-Day Life 68
The Synagogue 69
Signs and Symbols 70
Judaism and Children 71
Jewish Beliefs about Death 72
Jewish Prayer and the Sabbath 73
Pilgrimage, Food and Fasting 74
Jewish Festivals 75

Section Four — Islam

Basic Islamic Beliefs 76
Prophets and Angels 77
The Qur'an 78
The Prophet Muhammad 79
Different Islamic Traditions 80
Sufism 81
Islam and the Shari'ah 82
Islamic Living and Jihad 83
The Mosque 84
Worship and Prayer 85
Birth and Death Ceremonies 86

Published by Coordination Group Publications

Contributors:
Paul Cashman, Mark Chambers, Charley Darbishire, Julie Green, Gemma Hallam, Kevin Jones, Andy Park, Stephen Radford, Alice Shepperson, Moira Siara, Paul D. Smith, Nicola Thomas and David Walmsley

With thanks to Glenn Rogers, Dominic Hall, Katherine Reed and Glennis Atkinson for the proofreading

ISBN:1 84146 191 1
Groovy website: www.cgpbooks.co.uk
Jolly bits of clipart from CorelDRAW
Printed by Elanders Hindson, Newcastle upon Tyne.

Spirituality

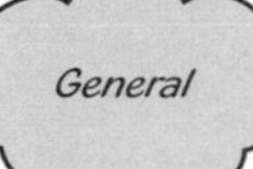

Q1 Which of these are spiritual questions?

a) What's for lunch?

b) Why are we here on this planet?

c) Why is it hot in summer?

d) Why should we try to be nice to other people?

Very nice.

Q2 Can non-religious people have spirituality?

Q3 A person of which religion might use a fish symbol to display their faith?

Q4 Give an example of how a Muslim woman might publicly show her spirituality.

Q5 *Douglas listens to a piece of music by Bach. He thinks the music is beautiful, and gets a strong sense of being on a "higher plane" when he hears it. Douglas is not a religious person, and the music is not religious music.*

Can Douglas' experience be considered spiritual?

Q6 Chaim is Jewish. He shows his spirituality by following the rules of the Torah. Give examples of two other ways that he might demonstrate his Jewish spirituality.

Q7 Explain two ways in which religious believers make external displays of their spirituality. (4 marks)

Q8 Give a brief explanation of how each of these terms can help to explain spirituality. (6 marks)

a) Meaning of life
b) Awe
c) Self-awareness

Q9 Describe how spirituality can be displayed through membership of a voluntary organisation. (6 marks)

Spirituality is like a butterfly — it's hard to pin down...

These probably seem like slightly weird questions — they're certainly not the sort of thing you'd get asked in a Science exam, that's for sure. Thing is, it's on the syllabus, so you have to know about it.

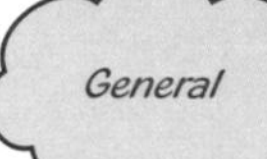

The Nature Of Truth

Q1 *There are different kinds of truth.* Write down the type of truth referred to in each of the following sentences.

a) "Scientists do experiments to test a theory."

b) "It's wrong to hurt other people's feelings."

c) "God created the world in exactly six days."

The nature of lies.

Q2 *Historical truth describes what happened in the past, using accounts from the past, and other sources (e.g. archaeology).*

Give two problems with using evidence to find out what happened in the past.

Q3 Can religious truth be proved to be true?

Q4 Read this description of a scene and answer the questions below.
The front room window of Mrs Smith's house is broken. There is a football in the middle of the room, surrounded by bits of broken glass. A child wearing football boots is standing in the garden, looking sheepish.

Evidence isn't the same as proof.

a) Is there evidence to suggest that the child broke the window?

b) *The child in Mrs Smith's garden says "We were playing football and my brother kicked the ball through your window. We're really sorry. Can we have our ball back".*
Does this mean that the brother definitely broke the window?

c) Is there any proof that either the child or his brother broke the window?

Q5 *People read holy books to look for spiritual truth.*

a) Give examples of books used to find spiritual truth.

b) Do all the people who find spiritual truth in the same book believe the same things?

Q6 *People use the advice of spiritual leaders and the Church to find truth.*

Why can this be an unreliable way of finding spiritual truth?

EXAM-STYLE QUESTION Q7 *"Holy Scripture is the only source of religious truth."*
Do you agree? Give reasons for your answer. Show that you have thought about more than one point of view. Refer to at least two religious traditions. (8 marks)

EXAM-STYLE QUESTION Q8 Discuss the importance of sacred books in Judaism, Islam and Christianity. (6 marks)

Believing in God

General

Q1 Are people brought up by religious parents more likely to be religious than people brought up by atheists?

Q2 *People turn to religion because they want answers to questions like, "Why are we here?".* Give two other reasons why people become religious.

Q3 *"Arguments from design" are sometimes used to justify belief in God.* Which of the following are arguments from design?

a) "The world is so complicated and intricate. It couldn't have got that way by chance."

b) "Mathematical truths are simple and beautiful. They must be meant to be that way."

c) "There is so much love in the world, and that love is proof of God's love."

Q4 Is everyone convinced by arguments from design?

"When I see all the glories of the cosmos, I can't help but believe that there is a divine hand behind it all." ***Albert Einstein***

Q5 How do scientific atheists and agnostics explain the following?

a) Miracles.

b) The range of living things in the world, all suited exactly to their habitat.

EXAM-STYLE QUESTION Q6 How might a belief in divine creation affect how a person thinks about life? (5 marks)

EXAM-STYLE QUESTION Q7 "We would not exist if we had not been created." Do you agree? Give reasons for your answer and show that you have thought about more than one point of view. (6 marks)

EXAM-STYLE QUESTION Q8 Explain why a person might convert to a religion. (6 marks)

Religious Experiences

Q1 What is a numinous experience?

Q2 What is a miracle?

Q3 Describe in a short paragraph how praying can help people to believe in God and to experience God.

Q4 Some Christians have "charismatic experiences". Give three examples of charismatic experiences that may take place during worship.

Q5 Who or what, according to many Christians, causes charismatic phenomena?

Q6 Some people focus their minds on God in order to have a close experience of the Divine. What is this process called?

Q7 *General revelation is something everyone can see.*
Special revelation is something that only an individual or select group can see.
For each of the following, write down whether it is a general revelation or a special revelation.

a) Reading the Qur'an.

b) Having a vivid dream of the prophet Elijah, in which he gives a specific message.

c) Meditating and having a vision of a saint.

EXAM-STYLE QUESTION Q8 Give a brief outline of a charismatic act of worship. (5 marks)

EXAM-STYLE QUESTION Q9 Explain how religious experiences may influence a person's faith. (7 marks)

Numinous — has nothing at all to do with numbers *(thankfully)*

There are different kinds of religious experience. Lots of religious people pray to God and read sacred books. Not everyone has visions or "speaks in tongues" — that's pretty rare, like a good Bruce Willis film.

The Nature Of God

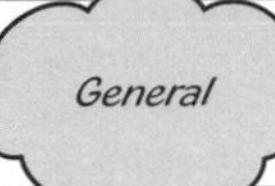

Q1 Do all religious thinkers agree that God is present within the Universe?

Q2 *Christians believe in a 'personal' God.* Answer these questions about belief in a 'personal' God.

a) Can someone pray to a 'personal' God?

b) Does a 'personal' God feel emotions like love and sadness?

c) What is the problem with the idea of a God who is personal, but also omnipresent (present everywhere in the Universe)?

Q3 What is meant by an **immanent** God?

Q4 What is meant by a **transcendent** God?

Q5 In Christianity and Islam, is God seen as outside the world, inside the world, or both at once?

Q6 Which of the following religions are polytheistic?

a) Islam

b) Hinduism

c) Christianity

d) Sikhism

e) Judaism

f) Old Norse and Ancient Greek religions

EXAM-STYLE QUESTION Q7 *"To experience God, a person must have a personal relationship with Him."* Do you agree? Give reasons for your answer. Show that you have considered more than one point of view, and include views from at least one world religion. (5 marks)

EXAM-STYLE QUESTION Q8 Explain how an immanent God can appear weak in the face of suffering within the world. (4 marks)

EXAM-STYLE QUESTION Q9 *"God is immanent and transcendent, personal and impersonal."* Do you agree? Give reasons for your answer. Show that you have considered more than one point of view. (8 marks)

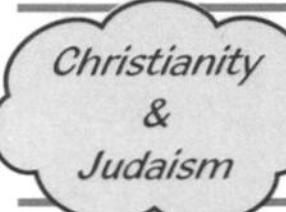

Christian and Jewish Teaching On God

Q1 Match each of the three descriptions of God below to the correct definition:

Omniscient	All-powerful.
Omnipresent	All-knowing. Knows everything you do and everything you think.
Omnipotent	Everywhere in the Universe at the same time.

Q2 *There's a big difference between Jewish and Christian ideas of God.*
What is the difference?

Q3 What does the Shema prayer say about the Jewish idea of God?

Q4 Answer these questions about the Trinity.

a) Who died on the Cross to save people from sin?

b) Which part of the Trinity is the Creator?

c) Which part of the Trinity is immanent, but impersonal?

Q5 *Many Christians believe in the Devil.*
What does the Devil do to humankind?

Q6 Is there a Devil in modern Judaism?

EXAM-STYLE QUESTION Q7 Explain what the Nicene Creed says about the Trinity? (7 marks)

EXAM-STYLE QUESTION Q8 Describe Christian beliefs about the Devil. (7 marks)

So there's one God... but there's also three...

Don't get your knickers in a twist... Christians definitely believe in just the one God — the Trinity just describes three different aspects. Make sure you know the differences between Christianity and Judaism.

Muslim Teaching On God

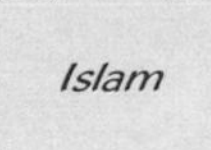

Q1 Is Islam a monotheistic religion or a polytheistic religion?

Q2 What's the literal translation of "Allah"?

Q3 *Muslims have many names for Allah.*

a) How many names does Allah have in the Qur'an?

b) Give four names for Allah that tell you something about Him.

Q4 *God can be seen as immanent or transcendent.*
Do Muslims see Allah as immanent, transcendent, or both?

Q5 According to Islamic teaching, has Allah intervened in human history?

Q6 Do Muslims believe that the Qur'an is the direct word of God?

Q7 How many prophets are mentioned in the Qur'an?

Q8 Who is the last of the prophets of Allah?

EXAM-STYLE QUESTION Q9 *"There is no way of knowing for certain what Allah is like."*
Do you agree? Give reasons for your answer and show that you have thought about different points of view. (5 marks)

EXAM-STYLE QUESTION Q10 Describe Muslim beliefs about Allah. (5 marks)

EXAM-STYLE QUESTION Q11 In what ways do Muslims seek to know Allah? (5 marks)

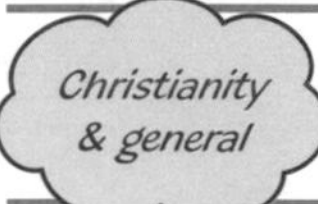

Evil and Suffering

Q1 Give an example of natural evil.

Q2 What kind of evil is murder?

Q3 *The division between human-made evil and natural evil isn't always clear cut.* Give an example of a disaster that is caused by human interference in the world.

Q4 *The existence of evil makes some people question their faith in God.*

a) How does evil damage the idea of an all-powerful God?

b) How does evil damage the idea of a God who answers prayers?

Q5 Explain how suffering can be a test of faith. Say how a person would pass the test.

Q6 Do Christians and Jews believe that evil was in the world from the start?

Q7 *After Adam and Eve ate the fruit of knowledge in the Garden of Eden, people were born imperfect and flawed.*

a) What is the idea of this flawed nature called?

b) What's this big change from perfect to imperfect called?

c) Was it up to Adam and Eve whether to eat the fruit of knowledge or not?

Q8 Who is Satan?

EXAM-STYLE QUESTION Q9 *"When people suffer, they deserve it for their own wrongdoing."* Do you agree? Give reasons for your answer showing that you have thought of different points of view. Refer to Christianity in your answer. (5 marks)

EXAM-STYLE QUESTION Q10 Explain how and why, according to Christianity, humans cause evil. Give examples in your answer. (4 marks)

EXAM-STYLE QUESTION Q11 How do Christians explain the origin and existence of suffering? (5 marks)

Judaism and Islam — Evil & Suffering

Judaism & Islam

Q1 Does Judaism say we have the free will to choose what to do, good or bad?

Q2 *The Book of Job demonstrates Jewish ideas about suffering.*

a) How does Job respond to his suffering?

b) Why does Job end up accepting his suffering?

A rare picture of Satan — caught taking a break between diabolical deeds.

Q3 *Judaism says that good can come out of suffering.*

Give two ways that this can happen.

Q4 *Some Muslims say that Shaytan (Iblis) tempts us.*

a) Why does Allah allow this?

b) According to Islam, do people have free will to give in to Shaytan or resist him?

Q5 Surah 2:214 of the Qur'an says, *"Do you expect to enter Paradise without being tested like those before you?"*

a) How does Allah test people?

b) What does the Qur'an say is the right response to Allah's test?

Q6 If a Muslim prays to Allah for forgiveness, will they be forgiven?

EXAM-STYLE QUESTION Q7 *"Good always comes from suffering in this world."*
Do you agree? Give reasons for your answer showing that you have thought of different points of view. Refer to Judaism in your answer. (5 marks)

EXAM-STYLE QUESTION Q8 *"Even the greatest suffering is part of God's plan for the world."*
Do you agree? Give reasons for your answer showing that you have thought of different points of view. Refer to Islam in your answer. (5 marks)

EXAM-STYLE QUESTION Q9 How do Muslims explain the origin and purpose of suffering? (6 marks)

"Surely We Shall Test You" (Brian Smith, Chief Examiner. 2003)

I know this book is causing you great suffering, but in the end, it will have positive results... trust me. It might not bring you closer to God, but it will help you pass your Exams. So that's evil done and dusted.

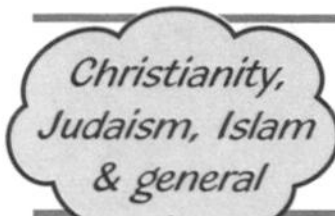

The Origin of the World

Q1 What is the main scientific argument for how the world began?

Q2 What is the main scientific argument for how living things came to be as they are today?

Q3 *The Bible says God created the world, the plants and animals, and Adam and Eve.*

a) Taken literally, does this idea agree with science?

b) Some people believe in both the religious and scientific explanations. How do they reconcile the two ideas?

c) In what order do these things appear in Genesis:
Space, people, the Earth, the atmosphere, plants, animals?

d) In what order does science say that these things appeared?

Q4 Do Orthodox Jews see the creation story in the book of Genesis as literally true?

Q5 Do Liberal Jews see the creation story in the book of Genesis as literally true?

Q6 Which holy book's creation story is the easiest to square with science — the Bible's story or the story in the Qur'an?

EXAM-STYLE QUESTION Q7 *"Science has already proved that God does not exist."* Do you agree? Give reasons for your answer showing that you have thought of different points of view. (5 marks)

EXAM-STYLE QUESTION Q8 What do Christians believe about the origin of the world? (6 marks)

EXAM-STYLE QUESTION Q9 Explain why some religious believers have more trouble than others in believing scientific theories about creation. (7 marks)

PLANET CONSTRUCTION TIP NO 112: *Shorten the trees — Don't stretch the animals*

Opinion is divided on how the world came into being. But I know how the world will end — I saw the film about the big asteroid with that famous bloke in. I'm pretty sure that was fact.

Life After Death

Christianity & general

Q1 What part of a person is believed to live on after death?

Q2 Does everyone believe in life after death?

Q3 *Some people who have been close to death (e.g. if their heart stops and is restarted) say that they have had near-death experiences.*

a) In a couple of sentences, describe a typical near-death experience.

b) Does everyone agree that near-death experiences are proof of life after death?

c) Give a non-spiritual explanation for near-death experiences.

Q4 Give another example of evidence for life after death, other than near-death experiences.

Q5 *Christians believe in Heaven.*

a) According to Christian teaching, what two things must a person do in order to go to Heaven?

b) What is the Communion of Saints?

Q6 Some Christians see hell as a real place full of fire and torment. Others see Heaven and Hell as states of mind. Briefly describe the "state of mind" version of Hell.

Q7 What is Purgatory? Which Christians believe in Purgatory?

Q8 Can people who have led sinful lives still be saved and go to Heaven?

EXAM-STYLE QUESTION Q9 Describe the Christian belief about what happens to people after they die. (7 marks)

EXAM-STYLE QUESTION Q10 *"Dead people's spirits can contact the living. This is proof of life after death."* Do you agree? Give reasons for your answer. Show that you have thought of different points of view. You must refer to Christianity in your answer. (5 marks)

EXAM-STYLE QUESTION Q11 Describe what Roman Catholics believe about what happens to the soul of a sinful person after death. (7 marks)

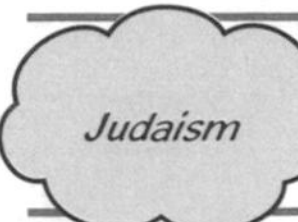

Jewish Beliefs about Life After Death

Q1 What is Sheol? What is it like in Sheol?

Q2 Briefly describe modern Jewish beliefs about Heaven and Hell.

Q3 Do Jews believe that non-Jews can go to Heaven and Hell?

Q4 *Many Christians say that only the soul goes to Heaven, not the body.*

What do Jews believe about what happens to the soul and the body after death?

Q5 *Thousands of years ago, in the time of the Bible, Jews believed that the sins of the fathers could be "visited upon the sons".*

What does this mean?

Q6 *Orthodox Jews believe that a person will still need their body after death.*

a) When will the dead person need their body?

b) Do Orthodox Jews cremate the dead?

c) Some liberal Jews cremate the dead. What do they believe about the body and the soul?

EXAM-STYLE QUESTION Q7 Describe what Orthodox Jews believe about what happens to good people after they die. (7 marks)

EXAM-STYLE QUESTION Q8 *"Jews are more concerned with this life than the afterlife."*
Do you agree? Give reasons for your answer. You must show that you have thought of different points of view. You must refer to Judaism in your answer. (5 marks)

Muslim Beliefs about Life After Death

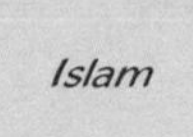

Q1 What is Akhirah in Islam?

Q2 What is yawm-ud-din (yawmuddin) in Islam?

Q3 What, according to Islam, are people judged on?

Q4 Briefly describe the Muslim Paradise.

Q5 Give the name for the Muslim Hell, and briefly describe it.

Q6 According to Islam, do we have free will?

Q7 How should a Muslim respond when bad things happen in his or her life?

Q8 *According to Islamic teaching, there's something that we humans know about our destiny that animals don't know.*

What is it?

EXAM-STYLE QUESTION Q9 Describe what Muslims believe happens to the soul after death. (8 marks)

EXAM-STYLE QUESTION Q10 Explain how Muslim beliefs about the afterlife affect the way Muslims live their lives. (7 marks)

EXAM-STYLE QUESTION Q11 Describe how Muslims believe a bad person can end up in Paradise. (4 marks)

I sentence you to 50,000 years community service...

Jews, Christians and Muslims all believe that people are judged after they die on how well they lived their life. Doing the wrong thing could have consequences that last for eternity — i.e. for ever and ever. Scary.

Christianity & general

Life & Death and the Christian View

Q1 Up until what week of pregnancy is abortion legal in England, Scotland and Wales?

Q2 *Doctors consider the quality of life of the pregnant woman when deciding whether she can have an abortion.*

Whose quality of life must they also take into account?

Q3 What does the Roman Catholic Church say about whether abortion is acceptable or not? Why does the Catholic Church say this?

Q4 Give two examples of situations where liberal Christians might say that abortion would be OK, even if they were against it on general principle.

Q5 What is the opinion of the Roman Catholic Church on contraception?

Q6 What is meant by the "sanctity of life" argument?

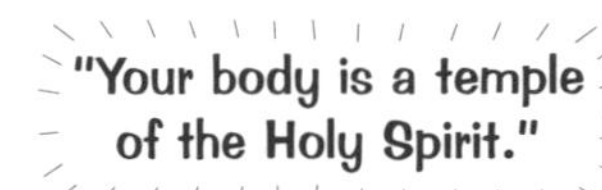

Q7 What's it called when an ill person asks for help to die?

Q8 Why might a Christian think that euthanasia could be the Christian thing to do in some circumstances?

Q9 Give one benefit and one danger to society of legalising euthanasia.

EXAM-STYLE QUESTION Q10 How might the teachings of Christianity influence a Christian when deciding what to do about an unwanted pregnancy? (6 marks)

EXAM-STYLE QUESTION Q11 *"What a woman does with her body is up to her. Abortion is her choice alone."* How might a Roman Catholic argue against this point of view? (5 marks)

EXAM-STYLE QUESTION Q12 Explain some of the arguments against the legalisation of euthanasia. You must refer to Christianity in your answer. (9 marks)

Life & Death in Judaism

Q1 For each of the following things, write down if Judaism generally views it as good or bad:

a) Abortion

b) Euthanasia

> "Be fruitful and increase in number... fill the earth." Genesis 1:28

Q2 *Contraception is often used by married couples for planning how many children to have and when to have them.*

Is using contraception in this way acceptable to most Jews?

Q3 Do all Jewish rabbis agree on abortion?

Q4 Is suicide a sin in Judaism?

Q5 *A doctor gives a lethal injection to speed the death of a terminally ill patient who is suffering a great deal.*

Is this considered wrong from a Jewish perspective?

> "There is no God besides me. I put to death and I bring to life." Deuteronomy 32:39

Q6 In Judaism, is it acceptable for a doctor to switch off a life-support machine or withhold life-extending treatment or food in order to speed the death of a terminally ill patient who is suffering a great deal?

Q7 Describe Jewish attitudes towards suicide. (6 marks)

Q8 A married Jewish couple are told by a doctor that any children they have are at a high risk of being severely disabled. Explain how Jewish teachings might influence their decisions about what to do. (6 marks)

Q9 *"Contraception and abortion are morally the same."*
Do you agree? Give reasons for your answer showing that you have thought of different points of view. Refer to Judaism in your answer. (5 marks)

Life & Death in Islam

Q1 Write down True or False for each of the following statements.

a) Islam teaches that life is a gift from Allah.

b) Islam teaches that we can decide when to end our lives.

c) Euthanasia is seen as wrong in Islam.

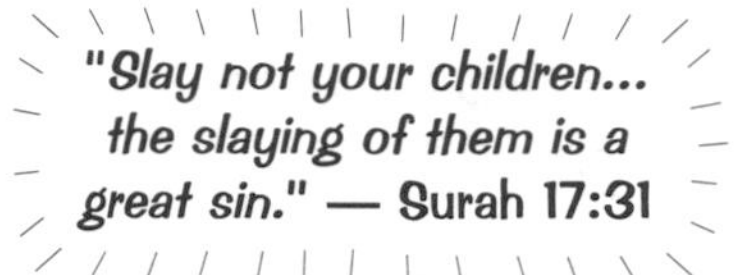

Q2 In Islamic teaching, when would abortion be seen as lawful and permissible?

Q3 Faiza has four children. She and her husband don't think that they could afford to bring up another one without their family sinking into poverty.

a) Would it be OK under Islamic law for the couple to use the Pill or condoms as a method of contraception? Explain your answer.

b) Would it be OK under Islamic law for Faiza's husband to get a vasectomy? Explain your answer.

Q4 *A Muslim couple have genetic testing done, and find that they have a greater than average chance of having children with cystic fibrosis (a genetic disease).*

Would it be acceptable under Islamic law for the couple to use contraception?

Q5 Is it acceptable in Islam to end someone's suffering by euthanasia?

Q6 How should suffering Muslims respond to their suffering?

Q7 Describe Muslim teachings about contraception. (8 marks)

EXAM-STYLE QUESTION Q8 Explain how a Muslim might respond to a suffering person who wanted to die quickly in order to end their suffering. (6 marks)

There's always two sides to an argument...

It's easy to learn how these religions view contraception, abortion and euthanasia — they're all bad. But they're badder in some circumstances than in others — you need to know all the stuff and all the biz.

Fertility Treatment

Christianity, Judaism, Islam & general

Q1 What is AIH?

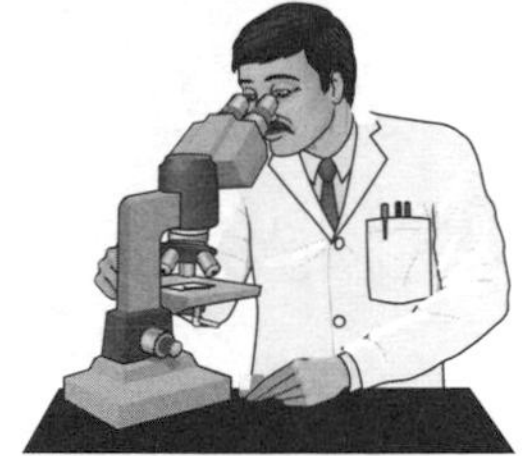

Q2 What is AID?

Q3 Explain why Christians, Muslims and Jews prefer AIH to AID.

Q4 In Britain, what happens to spare embryos from IVF (in vitro fertilisation) treatment?

Q5 Briefly explain why the Roman Catholic Church opposes IVF.

Q6 *Merav, who is Jewish, can't get pregnant. She asks her rabbi for advice on infertility treatment. The rabbi says infertility treatment would be a good thing.*

a) Why does Merav's rabbi says it's good for her to get treatment for her infertility?

b) What conditions might the rabbi place on egg donation, if it turned out that Merav and her husband needed it?

EXAM-STYLE QUESTION Q7 Describe how religious beliefs and teachings might influence a childless couple, when deciding what kind of treatment they will seek to help them conceive. (7 marks)

EXAM-STYLE QUESTION Q8 Explain why Jews and Muslims see artificial insemination by donor as an unacceptable method of treating infertility. (5 marks)

EXAM-STYLE QUESTION Q9 Describe the Roman Catholic approach to infertility and infertility treatment. (5 marks)

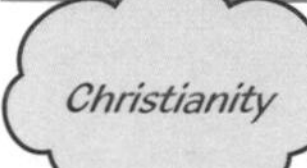

Marriage in Christianity

Q1 Compared to 20 years ago, are more or less people in Britain getting married?

Q2 Compared to 20 years ago, are more or less unmarried couples in Britain living together?

Q3 According to Christianity, what are two purposes of marriage?

Q4 Which of the following are genuine Bible teachings on marriage?

a) Husbands and wives must be faithful to one another.

b) Husbands and wives must share everything, including all the chores.

c) Marriage needs a lot of work, and husbands and wives must forgive each other.

d) The relationship between a husband and a wife is supposed to be like the relationship between Jesus and his followers.

Cheer up — you're getting married.

Q5 What is the Christian view on sex before marriage?

Q6 What happens during each of these parts of a wedding ceremony?

a) The declaration.

b) The proclamation.

c) The priest or minister's opening statement.

Q7 Describe what happens in a Christian wedding service. (8 marks)

Q8 Explain how religious beliefs and teachings might influence the sexual activity of a Christian throughout his or her life. (7 marks)

Q9 *"Sex is a sin outside of marriage."*
Do you agree? Give reasons to support your answer and show that you have thought about more than one point of view.
You should refer to Christianity in your answer. (5 marks)

The Christian Church and Divorce

Christianity

Q1 What is a nuclear family?

Q2 What is a reconstituted family?

Q3 In Britain, roughly how many marriages end in divorce?
Choose from one of the options below.

one in three   one in ten   one in thirty

Q4 *Christians don't all agree on divorce.*

a) Which branch of Christianity considers divorce to be impossible?

b) Why does this denomination believe that divorce is impossible?

Q5 What is an annulment?

Q6 *Claude and Iris are Catholics. They get married.*
However, Claude refuses to have sex with Iris on the wedding night (or indeed at all).

Can Iris get an annulment? Explain your answer.

Q7 What did Jesus say about remarrying after divorce?

Q8 Which of the following statements is true?

a) If you've been divorced, you can get married in any Protestant church.

b) If you've been divorced, you can't have a church wedding at all.

c) Some Protestant churches will let divorced people remarry, it depends on the minister.

EXAM-STYLE QUESTION Q9 Describe Christian beliefs about marrying again after a divorce. (8 marks)

EXAM-STYLE QUESTION Q10 *"People shouldn't divorce, but should work at the problems in their marriage."* Do you agree? Give reasons to support your answer. Show that you have thought about different points of view. Refer to Christianity in your answer. (5 marks)

Well, Elizabeth Taylor sure isn't Catholic...

You might have to discuss the pros and cons of divorce in the Exam, so be prepared. It depends on two things — Christian ideas about marriage, and Christian compassion for people having a hard time.

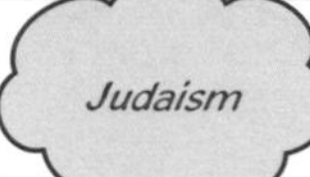

Marriage in Judaism

Q1 Which of the following statements is true?

i) Judaism sees sex as natural, God-given and holy.

ii) Judaism sees sex as dirty and tinged with sin.

Q2 How do Jews view the union between man and wife?

Q3 *Many Jews in Britain marry people who aren't Jewish.*

Why does this worry religious Jews?

Q4 What is a shadchan?

Q5 What is a ketubah?

"Ah, look how happy they are. I give it 3 years — tops."

Q6 *A Jewish wedding ceremony takes place under a cloth canopy.*

What is this canopy called?

Q7 Why does the bridegroom smash a glass under his foot?

Q8 What is a get?

Q9 *There are no agunot in Reform synagogues.*

Why is this?

EXAM-STYLE QUESTION Q10 Describe a Jewish marriage ceremony. (8 marks)

EXAM-STYLE QUESTION Q11 Explain how a Jewish woman can go about getting a religious divorce. (5 marks)

EXAM-STYLE QUESTION Q12 *"Marrying out is a threat to the Jewish people."*
Do you agree? Give reasons to support your answer.
Show that you have thought about different points of view. (5 marks)

Marriage in Islam

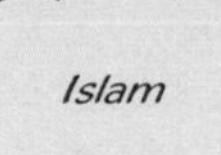

Q1 Was Muhammad a married man?

Q2 What does Islam teach about the sexual instinct?

Q3 Give two reasons why Muslims are advised to marry, other than to channel their sexuality appropriately.

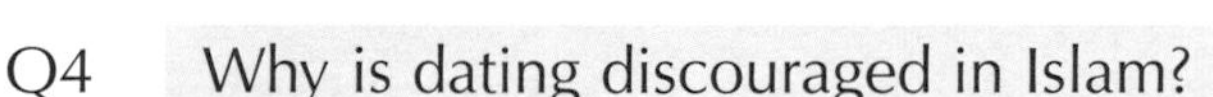

Q4 Why is dating discouraged in Islam?

Q5 Match each of the four features of a Muslim wedding below to the correct descriptions:

Nikah	A speech given after the marriage vows.
Mahr	The marriage contract.
Khutbah	A saying of Muhammad, read out after the marriage vows.
Hadith	Dowry — money paid by the groom to the bride.

Q6 Describe the quick way that a man can divorce his wife under Shari'ah law.

Q7 Answer the following questions about quick divorces under Shari'ah law.

a) Normally, how long is the "cooling off period" after the first declaration?

b) What's the Arabic name for this kind of divorce?

c) Can a British man divorce his wife in this way?

EXAM-STYLE QUESTION Q8 Describe Muslim teaching on divorce. (7 marks)

EXAM-STYLE QUESTION Q9 Explain how and why Muslim parents often choose marriage partners for their children. (7 marks)

EXAM-STYLE QUESTION Q10 *"The purpose of marriage is to provide companionship."*
Do you agree? Give reasons to support your answer and show that you have thought about different points of view. You must refer to Islam in your answer. (5 marks)

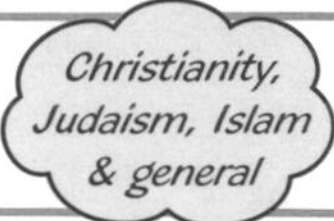

Religious Attitudes to Sex

Q1 What is the traditional religious view of sex outside marriage?

Q2 What is promiscuity?

Christianity, Islam and Judaism have a lot in common when it comes to attitudes towards sex — but they're not identical.

Q3 Is polygamy permitted in Judaism and Christianity?

Q4 How many wives may a Muslim man have?

Q5 Read the following paragraph, and answer the questions below:

Karim has one wife. He would like to marry a second wife.
Financially, he and his first wife are finding it hard to make ends meet.

a) Would it be OK by Islamic teaching for Karim to marry a second wife? Explain your answer.

b) If Karim did marry again, would it be OK for him to have a favourite wife and take her out on more dates than his other wife? Explain your answer.

Q6 What is the legal age of consent for homosexual acts between males in the UK?

Q7 Which of the following statements best describes the general Christian view of homosexuality?

a) "Homosexuality is a very bad sin, and should be condemned."

b) "There are no gay marriages, so all homosexual sex is outside marriage. For that reason, gay men and lesbians should be celibate."

c) "Homosexuality is the same, morally, as heterosexuality."

EXAM-STYLE QUESTION Q8 Describe Muslim teaching on polygamy. (6 marks)

EXAM-STYLE QUESTION Q9 Explain how Christian teaching might influence a gay Christian man's decision whether to have a sexual relationship with another man or not. (7 marks)

EXAM-STYLE QUESTION Q10 *"Religious beliefs about sex are out of touch with the modern world."* Do you agree? Give reasons to support your answer and show that you have thought about different points of view. (8 marks)

Children and Religion

Christianity, Judaism & Islam

Q1 Which of the following statements best sum up the Christian and Jewish ideas about how children should treat their parents?

a) Respect and honour your parents.

b) Get as much money and stuff from them as possible — you'll be looking after them one day.

Q2 Briefly write down what Islam says about how parents should treat their children.

Q3 According to Christian, Jewish and Muslim teaching, do grown up children have to look after aged parents?

Q4 Who is born a Muslim, according to Islam? Pick the right answer from the following options:

a) Everyone is born a Muslim, in submission to Allah.

b) No one is born a Muslim, you have to make the decision yourself.

c) Only the children of Muslims are born Muslim.

Q5 According to Christianity, can children be born Christian?

Q6 What conditions does a baby have to meet to be born Jewish?

Q7 Describe in a paragraph what Christians believe about the relationship between parents and children. (8 marks)

Q8 *"It is difficult to bring up children to be religious believers."* Do you agree? Give reasons to support your answer and show that you have thought about different points of view. (5 marks)

Children — they're the future of any religion...

I believe that children are our future. Teach them well and let them lead the way. Show them all the beauty they possess inside. Give them a sense of pride to make it easier. And so on.

Christianity & general

Prejudice and Equality

Q1 What is the legal principle of fairness called?

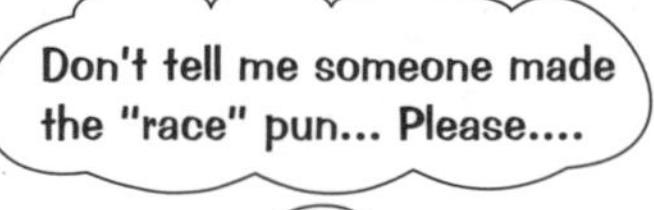

Q2 What is prejudice?

Q3 How can whole societies discriminate against groups of people?

Q4 Which of these is the most usual cause of someone's prejudice?

a) Direct experience of the group that the person's prejudiced about.

b) Ignorance and wrong beliefs about another group.

Q5 What is sometimes referred to as the "Golden Rule" in Christian teaching?

Q6 Why do Christians try to treat people equally?

Q7 Write down a brief outline of the story of the Good Samaritan.

Q8 *Colossians 3:11 says, "There is no Greek or Jew ...barbarian, Scythian, slave or free, but Christ is all, and is in all."*

What does this say about the Christian view of race?

Q9 a) Explain how Christian teachings might influence people's views on discrimination and prejudice in the world today. (5 marks)

b) Say how Christians could put those beliefs into use on a day-to-day basis. (4 marks)

EXAM-STYLE QUESTION

Q10 Explain what the parable of the Good Samaritan says about how Christians should treat people. (5 marks)

Race and Religion

Christianity & general

Q1 What are stereotypes?

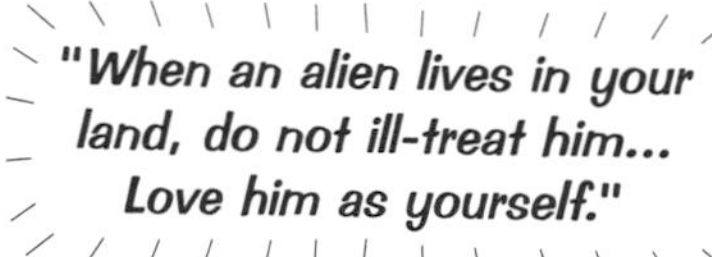

Q2 What is segregation?

Q3 In the UK, is it legal to draw up a shortlist of candidates for a job based on their race?

Q4 Briefly describe the view of today's Anglican Church on racism.

Q5 Which Church was partly responsible for the racist apartheid system in South Africa?

Q6 What is the name of the English bishop who fought apartheid, arguing that it was against God's will?

EXAM-STYLE QUESTION Q7 To what extent does British society today conform to Christian teachings about race relations? Give examples of racial prejudice and racial tolerance in today's society. (8 marks)

EXAM-STYLE QUESTION Q8 Explain how a Christian might use Christian teachings to argue against someone who had racist beliefs. (7 marks)

EXAM-STYLE QUESTION Q9 In what ways has the Christian church worked to combat racial prejudice? (5 marks)

Prejudice — It's nothing to be proud of...

As well as asking about how each religion sees racism and equality, you might be asked a general question about prejudice and equality in modern society. Don't get caught out — make sure you read the question.

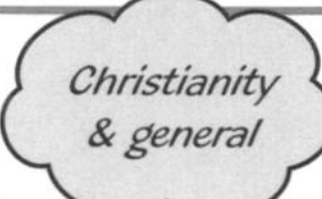

Injustice and Protest

Q1 In the UK, is it legal to discriminate on the basis of sex — e.g. by paying a man more than a woman for doing exactly the same job?

Q2 What was unusual about the fact that Jesus had female friends?

Q3 What does St Paul say about the position of women?

Q4 Why did the Nazis put a Christian called Dietrich Bonhoeffer in a concentration camp?

Q5 *Archbishop Oscar Romero spoke out against the government of El Salvador.*

What happened to him?

Q6 Name a Christian organisation that works against racism and injustice.

Q7 What are "prisoners of conscience"?

Q8 What is the name of the main charity that campaigns on behalf of "prisoners of conscience"?

EXAM-STYLE QUESTION Q9 Describe Christian teachings about the role of women in society. Are these reflected in British society today? (8 marks)

EXAM-STYLE QUESTION Q10 Describe the ways in which Christians have campaigned for human rights. (7 marks)

EXAM-STYLE QUESTION Q11 *"There's no use in pretending that people are equal."* Do you agree? Give reasons to support your answer and show that you have thought about different points of view. (5 marks)

Jewish Attitudes towards Equality

Judaism

Q1 In the Bible, the Jewish people are called "the Lord's people". Does this mean they're better than everyone else.

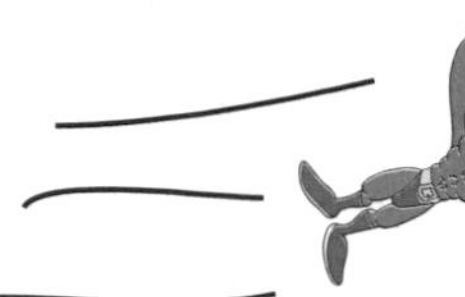

Q2 Ruth was a great hero of the Jewish people. Was she Jewish herself?

Q3 What is the traditional role of women in Judaism?

Q4 Which of the following statements describes an Orthodox synagogue?

a) Men pray downstairs. Women pray upstairs. The two sexes don't mix at the synagogue.

b) Men and women sit together. Women can read from the Torah.

Q5 Which branch of Judaism is least strict about the roles of men and women?

Q6 For Jewish services, a minimum number of people is required.

a) What is this minimum number called?

b) Can women make up this minimum number of people in a Reform synagogue?

EXAM-STYLE QUESTION Q7 Describe what Jews believe about the relationship between men and women. (8 marks)

EXAM-STYLE QUESTION Q8 Explain how a Jew might use Jewish teaching to argue against someone who had racist beliefs. (7 marks)

EXAM-STYLE QUESTION Q9 *"Jews shouldn't mix with non-Jews."* Do you agree? Give reasons to support your answer and show that you have thought about different points of view. (4 marks)

Muslim Attitudes towards Equality

Q1 Can people of any race be Muslims?

> ***"All people are equal...as the teeth of a comb. No Arab can claim merit over a non-Arab, nor a white over a black person, nor male over female."*** **Hadith**

Q2 What is the international community of Muslims called?

Q3 What is the Muslim view of racial discrimination?

Q4 How does the Hajj demonstrate equality between Muslims?

In a mosque, women and men must pray separately.

Q5 Does Islam say that men are created better than women?

Q6 What is the traditional role of women in Islam?

Q7 Were all of Muhammad's wives stay-at-home mums and housewives?

Q8 Explain why many Muslim women see wearing a veil (or hijab) and dressing modestly as liberating, rather than oppressing.

EXAM-STYLE QUESTION Q9 Describe Muslim beliefs about equality and unity. (7 marks)

EXAM-STYLE QUESTION Q10 Explain how a Muslim might use Islamic traditions and teaching to argue against someone who said that not all races are equal. (7 marks)

EXAM-STYLE QUESTION Q11 *"In a Muslim home, the husband must be the main earner."* Do you agree? Give reasons to support your answer and show that you have thought about different points of view. (5 marks)

Christianity and Other Religions

Christianity & general

Q1 Is Christianity today tolerant of other religions?

Q2 During which periods in history did Christians fight wars against Muslims for control of the Holy Land?

Q3 Which of the following statements best sums up the view of most Christians about other faiths?

a) All other faiths are untrue.

b) All faiths are equally valid — people should follow the faith that feels best to them.

c) Other faiths have some truth to them, but only Christianity has the whole truth about God.

Q4 What does evangelising mean?

Q5 Name a branch of Christianity which says it can and should try to convert everyone in the world.

Q6 Describe briefly what missionaries do.

Q7 What is the name for the idea that there's room for all religions, and that religions should show tolerance and understanding towards each other?

Q8 What does *The Inter-Faith Network for the UK* do?

EXAM-STYLE QUESTION Q9 Explain what is meant by the following terms, giving examples for each:
a) Religious exclusivity. (4 marks)
b) Religious pluralism. (4 marks)

EXAM-STYLE QUESTION Q10 Explain the attitudes of Christians to other world faiths. (7 marks)

EXAM-STYLE QUESTION Q11 *"Children must learn about other religions in school to combat prejudice."* Do you agree? Give reasons to support your answer and show that you have thought about different points of view. You must discuss Christianity. (5 marks)

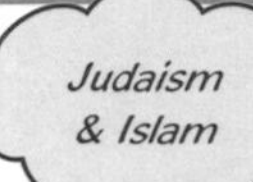

Judaism, Islam and Other Religions

Q1 In Judaism, is it considered OK for a person born Jewish to convert to another religion?

Q2 Do religious Jews try to convert non-Jews to Judaism?

Q3 What religious laws should non-Jews follow to be considered decent and righteous by Jews?

Q4 What does Islam say about Jews and Christians who believe in God and do the right thing in their lives?

Q5 Do Muslims try to convert non-Muslims to Islam?

"Those who believe in the Qur'an, and those who are Jews, and Christians — whoever believes in God and the Last Day and does right — surely their reward is with their Lord." Surah 2:62

Q6 What does Islam say about Jesus?

Q7 Name four prophets of Allah, other than Muhammad.

EXAM-STYLE QUESTION Q8 Describe Jewish views on other religions. (8 marks)

EXAM-STYLE QUESTION Q9 *"Jews, Muslims and Christians have so much in common that pluralism is the only sensible standpoint."* Do you agree? Show that you have considered more than one point of view. (7 marks)

Bill and Ted got it right — we should all be excellent to each other*

Basically, all three religions think roughly the same — we should all be tolerant of other religions and try to live together. But there are always those who take a more hard-line view. Make sure you learn the details.

*(and party on...)

Christianity and Poverty

Christianity & general

Q1 Give two examples of things that cause poverty in the Third World.

Q2 Give two examples of things that could make a family in the UK a lot poorer than the majority of families.

Q3 Is it considered OK for a Christian to make lots and lots of money?

Q4 Which industries does Christianity specifically frown upon?

Q5 If money belongs to God, should Christians try to redistribute wealth from rich to poor?

Q6 Give an example of a Christian agency which helps poor people.

Q7 Jesus said, "Whenever you did this for the least important brothers of mine, you did it for me."
How does this inspire Christians to do good works for charity?

EXAM-STYLE QUESTION Q9 Explain why some Christians disapprove of the National Lottery. (4 marks)

EXAM-STYLE QUESTION Q10 Explain why Christians might give money to charities. (5 marks)

EXAM-STYLE QUESTION Q11 *"Charity begins at home. Christians should help the poor in their own towns instead of sending money overseas."*
Do you agree? Give reasons to support your answer, showing that you have thought about different points of view. (5 marks)

Judaism, Islam and Poverty

Q1 *Judaism expects people to give money to charity to help the poor.*
According to Jewish teaching, what is the best way to help a poor person?

Q2 What are pushkes?

Q3 What is tzedaka?

Q4 What's the minimum percentage of wealth that a Jew should give to charity?

Q5 Is gemilut hasadim a good thing or a bad thing?

Q6 Which industries and lines of work should Muslims not work or invest in?

Q7 Why is it problematic for a Muslim to get a loan, when banks charge interest?

Q8 What is the 2.5% Islamic tax given to the poor and needy called?

Q9 What is sadaqah?

EXAM-STYLE QUESTION Q10 Explain the problems facing Muslims in a capitalist society. (8 marks)

EXAM-STYLE QUESTION Q11 *"It is wrong to be poor; it makes you a burden on society."*
Do you agree? Give reasons to support your answer, showing that you have thought about different points of view. Refer to Judaism in your answer. (5 marks)

EXAM-STYLE QUESTION Q12 How important is charitable work to Jews and Muslims, as part of living a righteous life? (5 marks)

Religion and the Environment

Christianity, Judaism, Islam & general

Q1 Give three examples of environmental problems in the world.

Q2 Give a reason why a business might choose a polluting way of doing something instead of a clean, green, non-polluting method.

Q3 Whose job is it to look after the Earth, in the opinion of Christianity?

Q4 Why is extinction of species worrying, from a Christian and Jewish point of view?

Q5 What do Jews believe about the position of humankind in creation?

Q6 According to Islam, when will we be called to explain how we treated the environment?

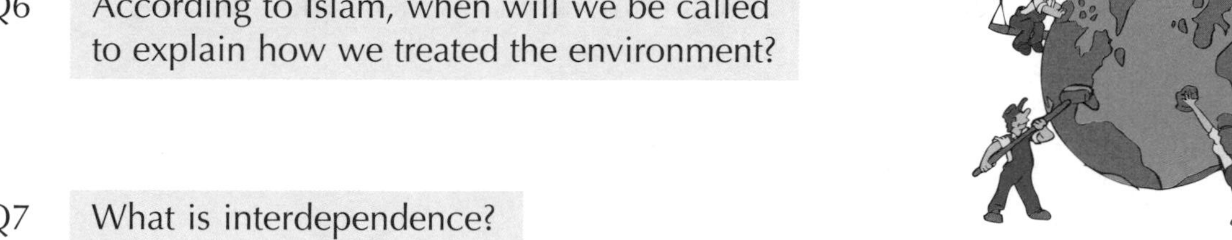

Q7 What is interdependence?

EXAM-STYLE QUESTION Q8 *"We are stewards of God's World."*
Describe Christian attitudes towards the natural world. (5 marks)

EXAM-STYLE QUESTION Q9 Explain how Jewish teachings might encourage someone to use "green" products, recycle waste and conserve energy. (5 marks)

EXAM-STYLE QUESTION Q10 *"God created the world, so it's God's job to look after it."*
Do you agree? Give reasons for your answer, and show that you have thought about different points of view. (6 marks)

Pollution is naughty — well, we can all agree with that...

With broad questions like, "Should we look after the environment?" you still have to know what different religions believe, and say <u>why</u> they support opinions either way. A load of <u>waffle</u> won't cut it.

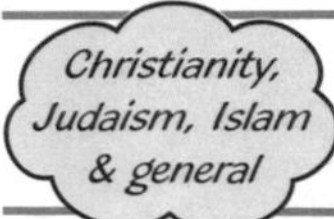

Religion and Animals

Q1 Are humans and animals equal in Christianity?

Q2 What is the relationship between humans and animals in Judaism?

Q3 What does Christianity teach about cruelty to animals?

Q4 Can a Christian be vegetarian?

Q5 Name a Christian denomination which is particularly opposed to hunting and animal circuses.

Q6 Name a Christian denomination which is generally more accepting of animal experiments than other denominations.

Q7 What is the Jewish view of medical experiments on animals?

Q8 How must animals for meat be slaughtered according to Jewish law?

Q9 What is the Islamic view of cruelty to animals?

EXAM-STYLE QUESTION Q10 Explain and compare Christian and Muslim attitudes towards animals. (5 marks)

EXAM-STYLE QUESTION Q11 Explain how religious beliefs might influence a woman's decision whether or not to wear makeup that had been tested on animals. (5 marks)

EXAM-STYLE QUESTION Q12 *"Religious believers should be concerned about people instead of animals."* Do you agree? Give reasons for your answer, and show that you have thought about different points of view. (5 marks)

Religion and Crime

Christianity, Judaism, Islam & general

Q1 Who enforces the laws of the land?

Q2 What is the difference between a sin and a crime, according to Christianity?

Q3 What is shari'ah?

Q4 What is a Bet Din?

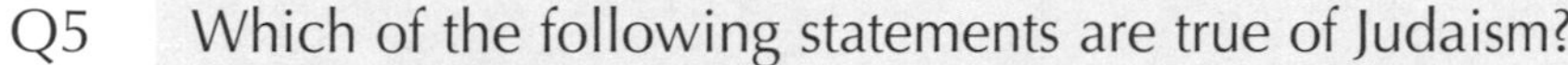

Q5 Which of the following statements are true of Judaism?

a) *"Jews must obey the 613 Torah laws first and foremost. The laws of the land are of secondary importance and can be broken."*

b) *"Jews must obey the laws of the land as well as the Torah laws in order to be considered righteous."*

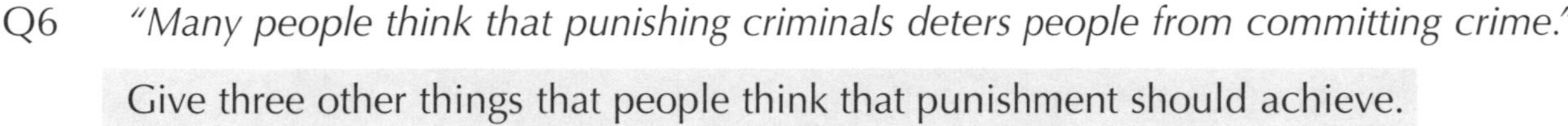

Q6 *"Many people think that punishing criminals deters people from committing crime."*

Give three other things that people think that punishment should achieve.

Q7 Can punishment deter people from committing crimes that aren't premeditated? Give a reason for your answer.

Q8 For what crimes does Judaism permit the death penalty?

EXAM-STYLE QUESTION Q9 a) Explain why some religious believers support capital punishment for some crimes. (5 marks)

b) Give a religious argument against capital punishment. (5 marks)

EXAM-STYLE QUESTION Q10 *"The main purpose of punishment must be to reform criminals."* Do you agree? Give reasons to support your answer, showing that you have thought about different points of view. (8 marks)

I say string them all up — not revising is a terrible crime...

Make sure you know the differences between a sin and a crime. In most countries, sins like adultery are not punishable by law — but in some Islamic countries, religious and state law are almost the same.

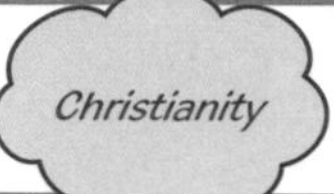

Christianity and War

Q1 What is the Christian view of war in general?

Q2 *"War must be declared by a proper authority."*

What is a proper authority?

Q3 Give an example of something that Christianity would consider a just cause for war.

Q4 *"Wars must be fought with discrimination."*

What does this mean?

Q5 What is a pacifist?

Q6 What is a martyr?

Q7 Give two examples of non-conventional warfare.

Q8 Why do Christian churches oppose nuclear weapons?

Q9 What is unilateral disarmament?

EXAM-STYLE QUESTION Q10 Describe what Christians believe about war. (4 marks)

EXAM-STYLE QUESTION Q11 *"Christians have the duty to end all wars and disarm all governments."* Do you agree? Give reasons to support your answer, showing that you have thought about different points of view. (8 marks)

Holy war, Batman — they've deployed God...

You might think that all war is wrong, but Christianity accepts that sometimes they have to be fought. This is why over the centuries the Church has laid down certain rules.

Judaism, Islam and War

Judaism & Islam

Q1 What does "shalom" mean?

Q2 What does "milchemet mitzvah" mean?

Q3 Which of the following are obligatory wars, according to Judaism?

a) A war to take over another country.

b) A war fought against a country that has invaded your own country.

c) A war fought against a country that you think is going to attack your country very soon.

d) A war fought against an enemy after negotiations have broken down.

Q4 Why are Muslims advised to "Hate your enemy mildly"?

Q5 What is Greater Jihad?

Q6 Which of the following are just wars, according to Islam?

a) A war to make people free from oppression.

b) A war to conquer a country and force the people there to become Muslims.

Q7 Who can declare a military Jihad?

Q8 What happens to someone who dies in a Jihad?

EXAM-STYLE QUESTION Q9 Describe what Muslims mean by 'Jihad'. (8 marks)

EXAM-STYLE QUESTION Q10 Explain how a Jewish government might respond to another country threatening to invade. Include Jewish teaching in your answer. (4 marks)

EXAM-STYLE QUESTION Q11 *"Sometimes, war is the only way of restoring peace."*
Do you agree? Give reasons to support your answer, showing that you have thought about more than one point of view.
You should refer to religious ideas in your answer. (5 marks)

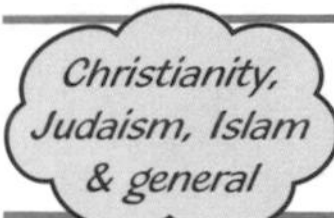

Religion and Drugs

Q1 Give two examples of hard drugs.

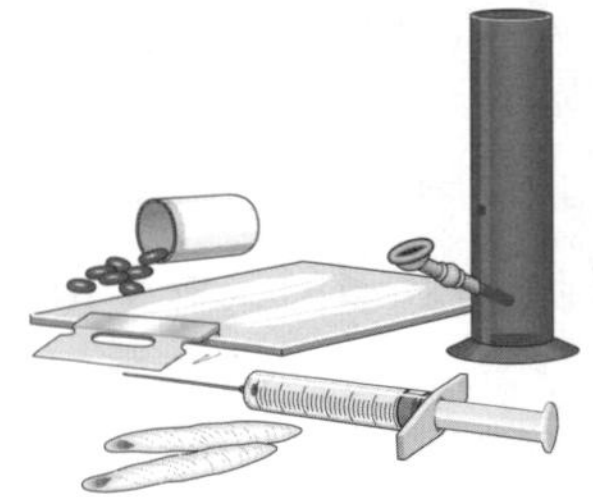

Q2 Give an example of a soft drug.

Q3 Give an example of a social drug widely used in British society.

Q4 *Christianity, Judaism and Islam all completely disapprove of illegal hard drugs.*

Give three reasons why all three religions disapprove of drug use.

Q5 For each of these religions, say whether alcohol is permitted in general, or forbidden.

a) Judaism

b) Christianity

c) Islam

Q6 What's the religious view of performance enhancing drugs in sport?

EXAM-STYLE QUESTION Q7 Explain why one main world religion forbids the drinking of alcohol, and why other world religions allow it. (8 marks)

EXAM-STYLE QUESTION Q8 The New Testament says, *"Your body is a temple of the Holy Spirit."* How does this affect the Christian view of drug abuse? (5 marks)

EXAM-STYLE QUESTION Q9 *"Cannabis and alcohol are both soft drugs. The Government should either legalise cannabis or make alcohol illegal."* Do you agree? Give reasons to support your answer, showing that you have thought about more than one point of view. Use religious arguments in your answer. (5 marks)

Oh no, not another lecture...

Don't say, "Drugs are bad, okay," and leave it at that — you have to put religious arguments in your answer too (it's a Religious Studies exam, duh). The faiths have pretty similar ideas, so it's not too hard.

Religion and the Media

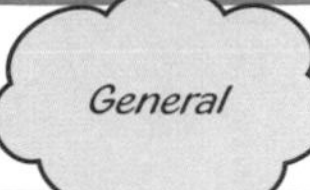

Q1 How has the number of people going to church changed over the last 50 years?

Q2 How have TV viewing figures changed over the last 50 years?

Q3 What does it mean to say that most broadcasting is secular?

Q4 Give two reasons why Jewish communities might be frustrated about the British media.

Q5 Give an example of a TV series that covers Muslim issues.

Q6 Give a reason why a religious person might be offended by soap opera characters and comedy characters.

Q7 What is the danger of relying on one newspaper for all your news and opinions?

Q8 Give an example of a book considered blasphemous by Muslims.

Q9 Why are some people concerned about allowing children to access the Internet freely? Give two reasons.

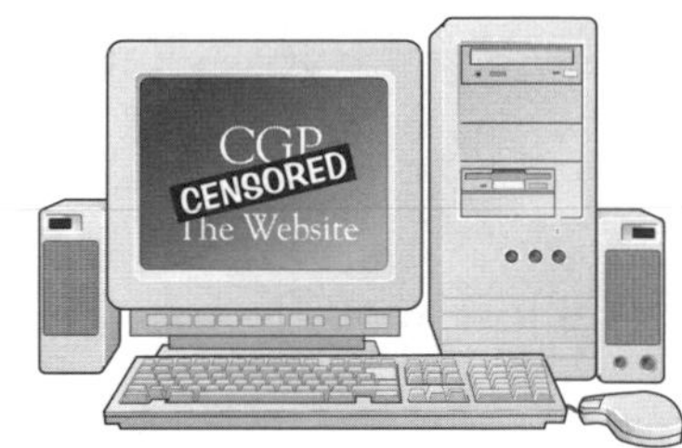

EXAM-STYLE QUESTION Q10 Explain why some religious believers dislike the religious programmes available on television. (4 marks)

EXAM-STYLE QUESTION Q11 *"There's no point in having a television. Television is immoral, and degrades people who watch it."* Do you agree? Give reasons to support your answer, showing that you have thought about more than one point of view. (5 marks)

EXAM-STYLE QUESTION Q12 Explain why some religious believers support censorship of the media. (6 marks)

Basic Christian Beliefs

Q1 What is the basic summary of Christian belief called?

a) Apostles' Screed b) Apostles' Creed c) Saints' Creed d) Apollo Creed

Not all Christians believe exactly the same things, but most accept certain basic doctrines.

Q2 *Christians say Jesus is "The Christ".* What does this mean?

Q3 Which of the following statements best summarises Christian beliefs about whether Jesus was human or God?

a) Jesus was all God. He was not human.

b) Jesus was a human. He was no more God than anyone else is.

c) Jesus was 100% human and 100% God at the same time.

d) Jesus was half human and half God.

Q4 How do Christians say that Mary, the mother of Jesus, got pregnant?

Q5 What is meant by "the Resurrection"?

Q6 Give two examples of how Christians symbolise the Holy Spirit.

Q7 How were humankind's sins atoned (paid) for, according to Christianity?

Q8 What do Christians believe will happen at the Last Judgement?

EXAM-STYLE QUESTION Q9 Describe Christian teachings about Christ's incarnation on Earth. (6 marks)

EXAM-STYLE QUESTION Q10 Explain why many Christians believe that Christ's death was the most important part of his ministry. (7 marks)

The Bible

Q1 For each of the following questions, answer either "Old Testament" or "New Testament".

a) Which part of the Bible is sacred to Jews?

b) Which part of the Bible contains the Gospels?

c) Which part of the Bible contains the Revelation of St John?

d) Which part of the Bible contains the Ten Commandments?

Q2 Whose example do Christians believe everyone should follow?

Q3 Give an example of a sacrament which appears both in the Bible and in modern worship.

Q4 Which branch of Christianity claims its authority from its teachings and traditions, as well as from the Bible?

Q5 What is: a) literalism?
b) fundamentalism?

Pastor Fred's "Sundaes on Sunday" Bible Study and dessert session went down a storm with the flock.

Q6 *Brian says that the Bible was inspired by God, but it wasn't directly dictated by God.*

a) What is the name for this view of the Bible?

b) Is Brian's view of the Bible rare in Christianity?

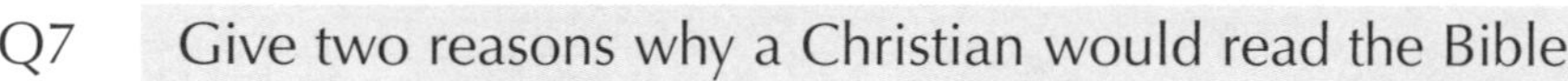
Q7 Give two reasons why a Christian would read the Bible.

Q8 Explain why the books of the New Testament (other than the Gospels) are important to Christians. (5 marks)

Q9 *"To be a good Christian, you must follow the teaching of the Bible."* Do you agree with this? Give reasons for your answer. Show that you have thought about other points of view. (5 marks)

Jesus and the Bible — you really HAVE to know this stuff...

This is all fundamental stuff — the kind of knowledge you can't get very far without. I mean, how can you answer questions about Christianity if you don't know what Christianity actually is... learn it all.

Christian Values

Q1 *Judaism teaches that 613 commandments from the Old Testament should be obeyed.* Which of these Old Testament commandments are most important to Christians?

Q2 Why did Jesus get into trouble for healing a man on the Sabbath.

Q3 Which were more important to Jesus — your actions or your intentions?

Q4 What did Jesus say was the most important commandment?

(Give yourself a pat on the back if you remember the exact wording without looking it up.)

Q5 Match the type of love to the description.

Eros	Christian love, like God's love.
Philia	Friendship, with give and take involved.
Storge	Sexual love.
Agape	Family affection.

Q6 Does Christian love involve keeping score, and making sure you take as much as you give?

Q7 What do Christians believe is the source of all love?

Q8 According to Saint Paul in his first letter to the Corinthians, which is most important?

a) Faith b) Hope c) Love

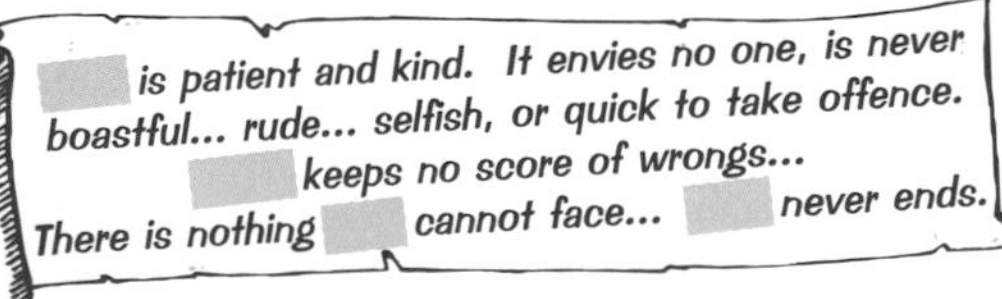

EXAM-STYLE QUESTION Q9 According to the teachings of Christianity, what should people do in order to be considered righteous at the Last Judgement? Refer to ideas about love in your answer. (7 marks)

EXAM-STYLE QUESTION Q10 *"The spirit of the Law is more important than the letter of the Law"* Do you agree with this? Give reasons for your answer, showing that you have thought about other points of view. You must consider Christianity and the Gospels in your answer. (5 marks)

Love and Forgiveness

Q1 What must we do to get God's forgiveness, according to Christianity?

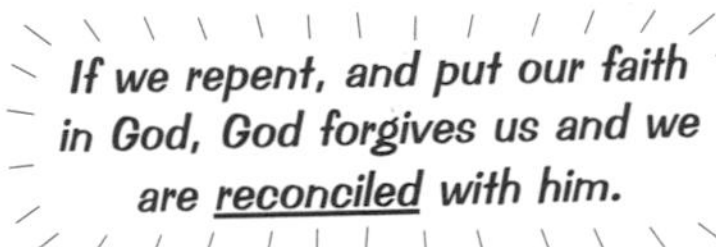

Q2 What does reconciliation mean?

Q3 What disadvantage do some people see to giving the poor lots of help?

Q4 Which of these is the most appropriate response for a Christian who has been hurt or wronged by someone?

a) Do nothing, and let the person hurt you again.

b) Sort out the problem, then forgive the person and move on.

c) Get revenge. Make the person sorry they ever thought about ticking you off.

Q5 Give three examples of things that Christians base moral decisions on other than Christian love.

"God forgives us our sins."

Q6 Is it necessary in Christianity to forgive each other, or is that only for God to do?

Q7 *Punishing criminals brings up plenty of dilemmas for Christians.*

a) Give a possible reason why a Christian might want to 'punish a criminal lightly'.

b) Give a possible reason why a Christian might want to 'punish a criminal harshly'.

EXAM-STYLE QUESTION Q8 Describe what Christianity teaches about the forgiveness of sins. (8 marks)

EXAM-STYLE QUESTION Q9 Explain why repentance is so important in Christianity. (7 marks)

Love is all around, it's everywhere I go — discuss...

Forgiveness is vital in Christianity, but even Jesus might have had trouble forgiving the British record-buying public for some of the shockers that have been Number 1 on his birthday. Take Cliff Richard... Mistletoe and Wine AND Saviour's Day. Then the Spice Girls... Christmas Number 1 for 3 years running (2 become 1, Too Much, and Goodbye). But at least we then had Bob the Builder... sanity clearly prevailed that year.

The Sermon on the Mount

Q1 What kind of people did Jesus say would "inherit the earth"?

Q2 What was the opinion of Jesus on doing good deeds in order to make people think you're a nice person?

Q3 Describe briefly Jesus' message about judging people.

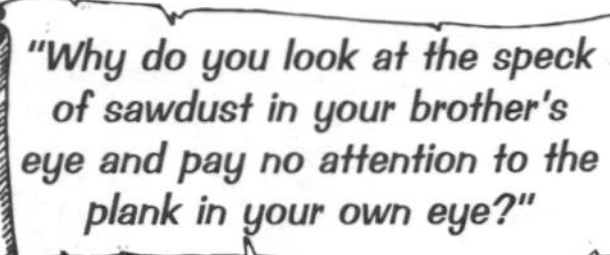

Q4 What is the Golden Rule that Jesus said summed up all the Law?

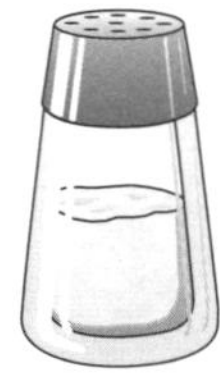

Q5 *Jesus said that people should be "the salt of the earth" and "the light of the earth".* Describe briefly what he meant.

Q6 Give an example of a Christian vocation.

Q7 What did Reverend Dr Martin Luther King try to achieve?

Q8 What did Mother Teresa of Calcutta try to do?

EXAM-STYLE QUESTION Q9 Describe what Jesus said about 'displaying religion' in the Sermon on the Mount. (4 marks)

EXAM-STYLE QUESTION Q10 Explain why Christianity teaches it's so important to serve other people. Give some examples of how Christians might choose to serve others. (6 marks)

Blessed is the Brian — for he shall act and shout a lot...

The Sermon on the Mount is probably THE most important sermon that Jesus gave. It's all there — the Golden Rule, judgement, sincerity, the Law of Moses, the Lord's Prayer and so on and so on.

Spreading the Gospel

Q1 What does "spreading the gospel" mean?

Jesus told his followers to '<u>spread the gospel</u>' (Matthew 28:19-20).

Q2 Write down two ways in which Christians can seek to challenge the society around them.

Q3 What is meant by "Christian apologetics"?

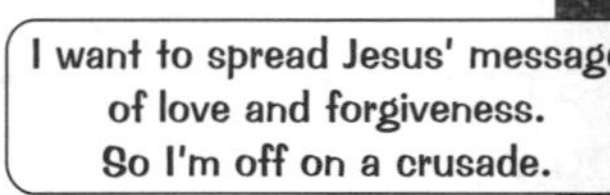

Q4 Why are Evangelical Christians so keen to convert people to Christianity?

Q5 What is absolute morality?

"If any of you is without sin... let him be the first to throw a stone at her."

Q6 What is relative morality?

Q7 Why do some Christians get involved with politics, and campaign about things like abortion and euthanasia?

Q8 Why are some Christians happy to stand back and let people make up their own minds on tricky moral issues?

EXAM-STYLE QUESTION Q9 Describe the importance in Christianity of spreading the Gospel. (5 marks)

EXAM-STYLE QUESTION Q10 Explain how Christianity might have an effect on politics in this country. (7 marks)

Living the Christian Life

Q1 *"Witnessing for Christ" is said to be the duty of every Christian.*
In what way do Evangelical Christians witness for Christ?

Practising Christians witness for Christ in different ways, depending on their denomination, culture, background, personal taste or talents.

Q2 What are "Alpha Courses"?

Q3 Suggest one reason why some Christians might find it difficult to explain their faith to other people.

Q4 *Christians can witness for Christ through their lifestyle.*
Suggest an area of their life where they might do this.

Q5 Give another way that Christians can 'witness for Christ' (apart from through talking to others, and through their lifestyle).

Q6 *Nuns and monks are members of religious orders.*
Some members of religious orders take three vows.
Name and describe each vow.

Q7 There are different kinds of congregation.

a) What are "contemplative congregations"? Give an example of one.
b) What are "apostolic congregations"? Give an example of one.

EXAM-STYLE QUESTION Q8 Describe how members of a particular religious community live their lives.
Why do this community's members live this way? (12 marks)

EXAM-STYLE QUESTION Q9 *"Spending your life shut away as a monk or a nun is a waste."*
Explain whether you agree with this, giving reasons.
Show that you have also thought about other points of view.
Refer to and explain any relevant Christian beliefs in your answer. (8 marks)

The Church

Q1 *St Paul said that the Church was the body of Christ.*

a) What is the aim or mission of the Church?

b) Who called the Church into being?

c) If the Church is the body, who is the head?

Q2 What is the name of the group consisting of all Christians who have died?

Q3 What is the name for work aimed at unifying all the different churches?

Q4 Whose teaching do Catholics follow on modern moral issues like abortion and contraception?

Q5 Who are the lay ministry and what do they do?

Q6 *Christians follow the teachings of the Church on ethical issues.*
Give examples of two other ways that the Church influences society.

Q7 Give three examples of ways that the Church puts Christian faith into action.

EXAM-STYLE QUESTION Q8 Explain how the Church influences and guides Christian believers. Make particular reference to the role of religious leaders. (7 marks)

EXAM-STYLE QUESTION Q9 Describe the role and function of a local Christian church. (7 marks)

Here's the church, here's the steeple...

It's pretty likely that you'll get some Exam questions about what the Church does and how Christians view the Church. It's pretty central as far as Christianity goes, so learn this stuff, plus the rest of the above rhyme.

Traditions and Denominations

Q1 Whose authority is most important to Protestants? Choose an answer from the options below.

The Church's   The Bible's   The Sacraments'

Q2 When did the Greek and Russian Orthodox Churches split from Roman Catholicism? What name is given to this split?

Q3 Which branches of the Church believe in the Seven Sacraments?

Q4 Which denomination holds worship services in silence until someone is "moved to speak"?

Q5 Which denomination has worship services with lots of singing, inspired by the Holy Spirit?

Q6 Explain the following terms: Magisterium   Dogma

Q7 What is special about pronouncements on morals that the Pope makes when he is sitting on his Papal throne?

Q8 *Catholics believe that Mary was born without any original sin (the sin that the rest of us are born with).* What is the name for this doctrine?

Q9 What is the doctrine of transubstantiation?

Q10 What is the aim of Liberation Theology?

EXAM-STYLE QUESTION Q11 Describe the main differences between Catholicism and Protestantism. (7 marks)

EXAM-STYLE QUESTION Q12 *"The similarities between different Christian traditions are more important than the differences"*
Do you agree with this? Give reasons for your answer, showing that you have thought about other points of view. (5 marks)

EXAM-STYLE QUESTION Q13 Explain why many Catholics try to follow the example of Mary. (6 marks)

Members of the Church

Q1 Who was the first Pope?

Q2 In the Roman Catholic Church, what's the next rank down from Pope?

Q3 Who appoints Catholic bishops? Choose an answer from the options below.

a) A group of cardinals.
b) All the priests in the diocese.
c) The Pope.

The ecumenical group discussed such matters as, "Milk first or tea first: What would Jesus do?"

Q4 What can priests do that deacons can't?

Q5 Who are the laity?

Q6 Where is a bishop's throne?

Q7 Who is the clergyman at the head of the Anglican Church?

Q8 Say whether priests in each of these denominations can marry.

a) Anglicans b) Catholics c) Greek Orthodox

Q9 Who appoints Presbyterian elders?

Q10 Who are patriarchs?

EXAM-STYLE QUESTION Q11 Describe the hierarchy of the Roman Catholic Church. (8 marks)

EXAM-STYLE QUESTION Q12 *"It is an important principle that Roman Catholic priests should remain celibate."*
Do you agree with this? Give reasons for your answer, showing that you have considered different points of view. In your answer, you must refer to the teachings of the Roman Catholic Church. (5 marks)

A Christian Church

Q1 Why were churches traditionally built in a cross shape?

Q2 Why do churches traditionally face east?

Q3 Look at this diagram and answer questions a)-c).

a) What is the purpose of this part of the church?

b) What are the two side wings called?

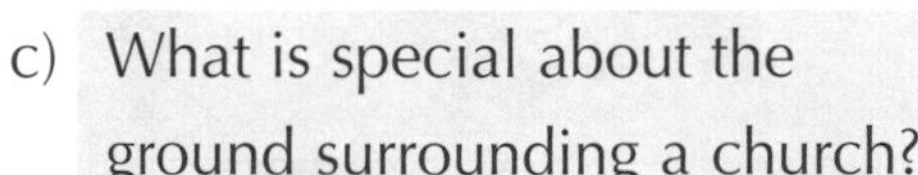

c) What is special about the ground surrounding a church?

Q4 Match the door or gate to the correct description of its use.

Porch	Large door used only for ceremonial occasions, e.g. when a bishop visits the church.
West Door	Where coffins are placed until the minister arrives to conduct the funeral service.
Lych-gate	Day to day entrance used by everyone.

Q5 What's the name for the part of the church where the congregation sits?

Q6 *Many Christian churches contain an altar.*

a) At what end of the church is the altar?

b) Name two denominations which don't have an altar.

c) Why don't those two denominations have an altar?

EXAM-STYLE QUESTION Q7 Describe the important external features of a church, and explain the function of each one. (8 marks)

EXAM-STYLE QUESTION Q8 Describe the important internal features of a church, and explain the function of each one. (8 marks)

Religious Symbolism

Q1 Why are cathedrals built so big?

Symbols are used to represent what's believed. Think of the cross — it's used to represent the sacrificial death of Jesus Christ.

Q2 *Orthodox churches have a dome on top.*
Describe the symbolism of the dome.

Q3 Why is the pulpit the focus of attention in a Baptist church?

Q4 Answer these questions about a particular branch of Christianity.

a) Which denomination has icons in its churches?

b) What do worshippers do to the icons when they enter the church?

c) What is the purpose of icons?

Q5 In what kind of church would you be likely to see dancing?

Q6 Why is music used in Christian worship services?

EXAM-STYLE QUESTION Q7 Describe the religious symbolism in Orthodox churches. (8 marks)

EXAM-STYLE QUESTION Q8 Explain the ways in which a sense of awe and wonder might be inspired in a cathedral. (6 marks)

I got a sense of awe in a cathedral — it cost a fortune to get in...

There's all kinds of symbolism in Church buildings and services of worship. Rather interesting if you're into that sort of thing. And even if not, you might still have to answer a question on it in the Exam.

Sunday Worship

Q1 On what day of the week would Jesus, as a Jew, have celebrated the Sabbath?

Q2 Give two reasons why Christians observe the Sabbath on a Sunday.

Q3 What does it mean to say that a service is "liturgical"?

Not all of Jesus' utterances at the Last Supper are equally famous.

Q4 What did Jesus say about the bread and wine at the Last Supper?

Q5 What do Roman Catholics believe about the bread and wine of Communion?

Q6 What happens to leftover consecrated bread and wine?

Q7 Put these parts of the Mass in the right order.

Penitential Rite	Readings
Rite of Communion	Eucharistic Prayers

Q8 What happens during each of these parts of the Mass?

a) Penitential Rite

b) Eucharistic Prayers

EXAM-STYLE QUESTION Q9 Describe what happens at a Catholic Mass. (8 marks)

EXAM-STYLE QUESTION Q10 *"Holy Communion is the most important way for Christians to worship."*
Do you agree with this? Give reasons for your answer.
Show that you have thought about other points of view. (5 marks)

Christian Festivals

Q1 When does Advent begin?

Q2 Which of the following is the first day of Lent?

a) Shrove Tuesday b) Ash Wednesday c) Maundy Thursday

Q3 What do each of the following festivals commemorate?

a) Epiphany

b) Palm Sunday

c) Pentecost

Q4 What is the transfiguration?

Q5 Why do people put ash on their foreheads on Ash Wednesday?

Q6 What is the name of the feast that marks Jesus going to Heaven?

Q7 Mary is a central figure in some branches of Christianity.

a) What do Catholic and Orthodox Christians believe happened to Mary, mother of Jesus, at the end of her earthly life?

b) What day of the year is the feast day dedicated to Mary?

EXAM-STYLE QUESTION Q8 Describe what Christians might do to get ready spiritually for Easter. (8 marks)

EXAM-STYLE QUESTION Q9 *"There's no point in having Advent when shops start Christmas in September."* Do you agree with this? Refer to Christianity in your answer, giving reasons. Show that you have thought about other points of view. (5 marks)

Pancake Day — a fine tradition worth upholding...

Hard though it may be to believe, Christmas has something to do with religion. Easter too. Well, it must be true what they say — you learn something new every day. But anyway... just remember the famous parable about Jesus and the Easter Bunny going to the North Pole to get their toys from Santa, and you'll be okay.

Private Prayer and the Sacraments

Q1 What is a contemplative prayer?

Q2 a) What is the rosary?

b) Name two prayers said using the rosary.

Q3 Which of the following are Sacraments in the Catholic Church?

a) Birth	d) Tea and biscuits
b) Marriage	e) Redemption
c) Ordination	f) Reconciliation

Q4 a) Give another name for the anointing of the sick.

b) What are the sick anointed with?

Q5 In the sacrament of reconciliation, what must follow after the person confesses their sin to the priest?

Q6 Which sacraments are accepted by mainstream Protestants?

Q7 Which of the following statements best sums up the Catholic and Anglican view of Sacraments?

a) "Sacraments are only special because they're special times in a Christian's life."	b) "Sacraments are so special because the grace of God enters into a person through the Sacrament."

EXAM-STYLE QUESTION Q8 Describe the Christian sacraments and how they are viewed by different branches of the Church. (8 marks)

EXAM-STYLE QUESTION Q9 Describe two different kinds of private prayer. (4 marks)

Baptism

Q1 Who baptised Jesus?

Q2 When did Jesus tell his disciples that they should baptise people?

"Go and make disciples of all nations, baptising them in the name of the Father, Son and Holy Spirit."

Q3 Baptism is an important rite in Christianity.

a) Why do Baptists and Pentecostal Christians only baptise Christian believers (who will be young teens and upwards) rather than babies?

b) Why do Catholics, Orthodox and Anglicans think it's good to baptise babies?

Q4 Who makes promises to be a good Christian on behalf of a baby being baptised?

Q5 What's the name of the water container over which the baby is baptised?

Q6 Why do parents and godparents hold a candle?

Q7 When do Catholic children have their first Communion?

Q8 Describe what happens at the baptism of an adult believer.

EXAM-STYLE QUESTION Q9 Explain the significance of baptism in Christianity. (7 marks)

EXAM-STYLE QUESTION Q10 Describe what happens at the baptism of a baby. (5 marks)

EXAM-STYLE QUESTION Q11 *"Babies must be baptised."*
Do you agree with this? Give reasons for your answer.
Show that you have thought about other points of view. (5 marks)

Baptism — go on, dive straight into the topic...

Baptism is one of just two sacraments (direct grantings of God's grace) accepted by both Protestants and Catholics, so it must be important. And prayer — what do you reckon... important or not...

Funerals, Burials and Cremation

Q1 Who do Christians believe can be resurrected after they die?

Q2 What does the Christian Church believe about sin, God's standards of behaviour, and going to Heaven?

Q3 What does the Christian Church believe Jesus did to the link between sin and death?

Q4 Give an example of a New Testament verse that is commonly read at funeral services.

Q5 Why doesn't it matter if the body is cremated?

Q6 What is a Requiem Mass for?

Q7 What is the name of the white cloth that covers the coffin during a Requiem Mass?

Q8 How can the funeral service sometimes help the bereaved person?

Q9 What can priests and vicars do to try and comfort the bereaved?

EXAM-STYLE QUESTION Q10 Describe a Christian burial service. (8 marks)

EXAM-STYLE QUESTION Q11 Explain how Christians might comfort someone whose close friend has recently died. (4 marks)

Christianity tries to view death in a positive way...

Death is usually a very upsetting time for those left behind, but Christians try to take comfort from the fact that the person who died has gone to Heaven (hopefully). It can make an upsetting time easier to cope with.

Jesus and Mark's Gospel

Q1 Which 3 Gospels are the Synoptic Gospels?

Christians consider the Gospels to be Scripture (holy writings inspired by God).

Q2 When do people think that Mark's Gospel was written?

Q3 Do people think that Mark knew Jesus himself?

Q4 Give three times from Mark's Gospel where Jesus is called the Son of God.

Q5 Which Old Testament prophet wrote about a Son of Man who would have authority from God?

Q6 Give another title that means the same as Messiah.

Q7 What is the significance of the woman at Bethany pouring perfume on Jesus' feet?

Q8 Who is the first person to call Jesus Son of David in public, without being criticised or shouted down.

Q9 When in Mark's Gospel does Jesus save a Gentile (a non-Jew)?

EXAM-STYLE QUESTION Q10 Give two titles used for Jesus from Mark's Gospel, and explain the significance of each. (4 marks)

EXAM-STYLE QUESTION Q11 Explain what is meant by 'Messiah'. Describe the different attitudes that are shown in Mark's Gospel regarding Jesus as the Messiah. (6 marks)

The Kingdom of God

Q1 *The Pharisees asked Jesus when he believed that the Kingdom of God would come.* What was Jesus' answer?

Q2 When did Jesus say, "The Kingdom of God is at hand."

Q3 What did Jesus mean when he said that people should approach the Kingdom of God "like a little child"?

Q4 What did Jesus say about being rich and going to Heaven?

Tricky... but not impossible.

Q5 What do the parables of the *growing seed* and the *mustard seed* (4:26-32) say about the Kingdom of God?

Q6 In the parable of the vineyard:

a) Who is represented by the vineyard owner?

b) Who are the tenants of the vineyard supposed to be?

Q7 What does the parable of the lamp say about Jesus?

Q8 Give an outline of the parable of the vineyard, and explain its significance. (8 marks)

Q9 Explain Jesus' teachings about the Kingdom of God. (7 marks)

EXAM-STYLE QUESTION Q10 *"Jesus confused people by talking in parables. He should have said what he meant."* Do you agree with this? Give reasons for your answer. Show that you have thought about other points of view. (5 marks)

Before you go learning all this stuff, just pause for a moment...

There's a load of stuff that you might need to learn in Mark's Gospel — but it's not included on all syllabuses. So before you get too carried away with committing all this stuff to memory, it's probably a good idea to check that you actually need to know it. You might need the brain-space for other things.

Jesus and Miracles

Q1 Give an example of Jesus calming Nature.

Jesus' miracles involved controlling nature and curing mental and physical illness.
He performed miracles to show had God's power and to demonstrate the importance of faith.

Q2 What happened at the feeding of the 5000?

Q3 In the story of the man possessed by many evil spirits, where did Jesus send all the spirits?

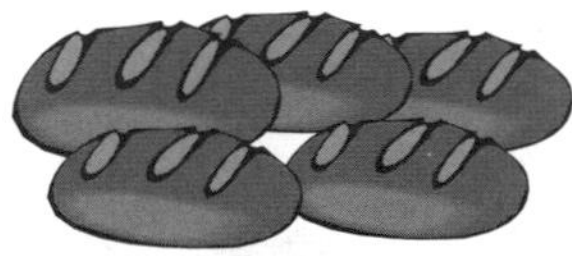

Q4 Give four examples of the types of illness and disability that Jesus cured.

Q5 *Jesus asked some folk to keep quiet about the miracles, and asked others to spread the news.* Give an example of a healing miracle that Jesus asked to be kept quiet.

Q6 Why was Jesus accused of blasphemy when he healed the paralysed man? Choose the correct answer from the options below:

a) Because God obviously meant the man to be paralysed.

b) Because the crowd thought it was witchcraft.

c) Because he also forgave the man his sins, and the crowd said that only God can forgive sins.

EXAM-STYLE QUESTION Q7 Describe one of Jesus' nature miracles, and explain its significance in Christianity. (6 marks)

EXAM-STYLE QUESTION Q8 *"Jesus' miracles were impossible. They never really happened."* Do you agree with this? Give reasons for your answer. Show that you have thought about other points of view. (5 marks)

Don't rely on miracles to pass your Exams...

Jesus performed many miracles — he believed nothing was impossible. Although to be fair, he never tried to get put through to a human operator on a Customer Helpline. Feeding the 5000 was probably relatively easy.

Miracles, Faith and Conflict

Q1 In the story of Jairus' daughter, how does Jairus show he has faith?

Q2 *In Mark 5:25-34, Jesus heals a woman who touches his cloak.*

a) Does Jesus know which person in the crowd touched his cloak?

b) How does Jesus explain the woman's healing?

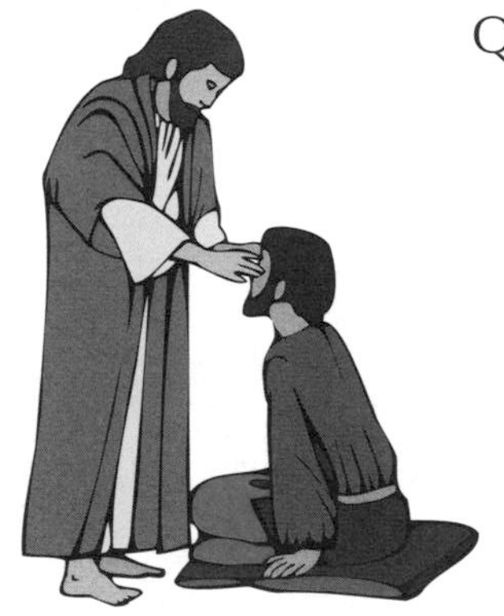

Q3 Faith is an important part of any religion.

a) According to Jesus' healing miracles in the Gospel of Mark, is it enough to sit back and trust God to 'sort it all out'?

b) If not, what do people have to do as well?

Q4 Give an example of a time when the disciples failed to cure a sick person, and explain why they failed.

Q5 What did Jesus say to the Pharisees about paying tax?

Q6 What did Jesus say to the Pharisees about the ritual washing laws?

Q7 Give an example of a time when the disciples were accused of breaking Sabbath laws.

EXAM-STYLE QUESTION Q8 Explain the difference between Jesus' attitude towards religious rituals and those of the Pharisees. (7 marks)

EXAM-STYLE QUESTION Q9 What do healing miracles show about the relationship between Jesus and the people he healed? (5 marks)

EXAM-STYLE QUESTION Q10 *"Christians have a duty to challenge authority."* Do you agree with this? Give reasons for your answer. Show that you have thought about other points of view. (5 marks)

Discipleship

Q1 *Jesus gathered his disciples and sent them off on a mission.*

a) Who or what did Jesus give the disciples authority over?

b) Give two examples of things that the disciples were not allowed to take with them.

c) What did Jesus say the disciples were to do when they were made unwelcome?

Q2 What did Jesus mean about his ministry when he said that healthy people didn't need a doctor?

"Whoever does God's will is my brother and sister and mother."

Q3 *Peter said he'd tell people that Jesus is the Christ.* What did Jesus tell Peter to do?

Q4 Which of the following are qualities that a disciple should have?

a) Must speak Greek

b) Must love kids

c) Must be faithful to husband or wife

d) Must not eat meat

e) Must make financial sacrifices

f) Must preach the Gospel

Q5 Which story gives the example of making financial sacrifices and digging deep in your pockets to make offerings?

Q6 According to the Gospel of Mark, how much bigger are the rewards of discipleship than the costs?

EXAM-STYLE QUESTION Q7 Describe what Jesus taught his disciples about serving others. (4 marks)

EXAM-STYLE QUESTION Q8 *"You can't have a house and possessions if you're a disciple of Jesus."*
Do you agree with this? Give reasons for your answer.
Show that you have thought about other points of view. (5 marks)

Discipleship has its ups and its downs...

There's actually a version of the Bible written in Cockney rhyming slang. In fact, historians now believe that this is how Jesus spoke most of the time. *"I've come to heal the Tom and Dick..." "Why do you look at the speck of sawdust in your brother's mince pie..." "Accept the Kingdom of God like a dustbin lid..." "Those who Adam and Eve in me will never be brown bread..."* and I could go on. Make sure you learn them.

Jesus' Trial and Death

Q1 The Last Supper was a meal to celebrate which Jewish festival? Choose an answer from the options below.

a) Shavuot	c) Purim
b) Sukkot	d) Passover

Q2 a) At the Last Supper, what did Jesus foretell about betrayal?

b) What did Jesus foretell about someone denying that they knew him?

Q3 *Jesus was tried by a religious court.*

a) Where was the religious trial held?

b) Did the prosecution witnesses agree with each other?

Q4 Why did the people of Jerusalem tell Pilate to release Barabbas (a murderer) instead of Jesus?

Q5 What did the sign on Jesus' cross say?

Q6 What were Jesus' last words?

Q7 Who gave the news of Jesus' resurrection to the disciples?

Q8 Describe what Jesus told the disciples when he appeared to them after his resurrection.

EXAM-STYLE QUESTION Q9 Explain why the crucifixion and resurrection are so important to Christians. (6 marks)

EXAM-STYLE QUESTION Q10 Give an outline of Mark's account of the Last Supper. (6 marks)

Kind of the whole point of Christianity, this...

There's a lot to learn and remember about the crucifixion and resurrection. You can be asked to retell the whole crucifixion story, or the whole Last Supper story, so get those details well and truly learned.

The Beginnings of Judaism

Q1 Describe how Abraham's beliefs about God were very different from those of the people of Ur.

Q2 Where did God tell Abraham to go and live?

Q3 Why did Abraham's descendants go to Egypt?

Q4 For how long were the descendants of Abraham (the Jews) slaves of the Egyptians?

Q5 *The Jews were led out of Egypt and back to freedom.*

a) Who led the Jews out of Egypt?

b) How long did it take the Jews to get from Egypt back to the Promised Land?

Q6 Where did Moses receive the 10 commandments?

Q7 Why did the Jewish tribes ask God to give them a king?

Q8 Who built the first permanent Temple in Jerusalem?

Q9 *Jewish beliefs are based around the idea of a covenant with God.*

a) What did God promise Abraham in the covenant?

b) What did Abraham have to promise in return?

Q10 When do Jews believe that the whole of Israel will be theirs to live in?

EXAM-STYLE QUESTION Q11 Describe the giving of the Covenant to Abraham and the renewing of the Covenant with Moses. (6 marks)

EXAM-STYLE QUESTION Q12 Describe Jewish beliefs about the Promised Land. (7 marks)

Whoa-oa — the Israelites...

You've heard of Moses... you know that there's 10 Commandments... the name David rings a bell — well that's not good enough come the Exam. You need to know all this stuff like the back of your hand.

Basic Jewish Beliefs

Q1 Which of the following are believed by most Jews?

> There is only one God. God denies people free will.
> God is a 'force' — not a person. God's energy keeps the Universe going.

Q2 What is the name of the prayer which starts,
"Hear O Israel: the Lord our God, the Lord is One"?

Q3 Why do Jews refer to God as Hashem and Adonai?

Q4 Why do Jews believe that God chose them to be his special people?

Q5 What is Zionism?

Q6 *The Jewish people have been evicted from Israel at several points in history.*

a) When were the Jews exiled to Babylon?

b) Who destroyed Jerusalem in 70CE?

c) What is the name for the time when Jews couldn't live in Israel?

Q7 When was the modern state of Israel established?

Q8 Give a religious reason why some Jews disagreed with the establishment of the state of Israel.

Q9 Describe Jewish beliefs about the nature of God. (8 marks)

EXAM-STYLE QUESTION Q10 Describe the special role that Jews believe they have in the world, and why. (5 marks)

Sources of Guidance

Q1 What is the Tenakh?

Q2 Write down the Hebrew word for each of the following:

a) The books of the Prophets

b) The books of the Law

c) The books of psalms, proverbs and philosophy

Q3 Give the names of two prophets whose writings are found in the "Latter Prophets" part of the Tenakh.

Q4 *There are lots of teachings which help Jews to interpret the Torah. Many of these were originally passed on by word of mouth, and were written down later.*

a) Who wrote down the Mishnah?

b) What is the Gemara?

c) What is the name for the Mishnah and Gemara together?

Q5 What is Halakhah?

Q6 *Modern technology raises new and tricky questions for Jews.* How do modern Jews decide how to use technology in a way that doesn't break any Torah laws?

Q7 A Bet Din can play an important role in Jewish life.

a) What is a Bet Din?

b) Give examples of three kinds of dispute that a Bet Din might sort out.

EXAM-STYLE QUESTION Q8 Describe what is in the Tenakh. (6 marks)

EXAM-STYLE QUESTION Q9 Explain why the Talmud is so important. (7 marks)

EXAM-STYLE QUESTION Q10 *"The Torah is so old it is impossible to apply it to modern life."* Do you agree with this? Refer to Judaism in your answer, giving reasons. Show that you have thought about other points of view. (5 marks)

Torah — didn't she have a few hits in the early 80s...

The 'Jewish Bible' is pretty much the same as the Christian Old Testament. But that's not the only source of religious guidance in Judaism — there are a few other collections of teachings you need to know about too.

The Holocaust

Q1 What is anti-Semitism?

Q2 Who did the National Socialist Party of Germany (the Nazi party) blame for Germany's problems?

Q3 What did Hitler and the other Nazi leaders call the plan to kill all the Jews in Europe?

Q4 Roughly how many Jews were killed by the Nazis during the Holocaust?

Q5 Give two examples of tricky theological and philosophical questions raised by the events of the Holocaust.

Q6 Explain why the Holocaust has caused some Jews to become atheist (i.e. they have concluded that there cannot be a God).

Q7 Why do some people think it would be impossible for God to destroy all evil people and save all good people?

Q8 Why do some Jews think that since the Holocaust, it's more important than ever to keep practising Judaism?

EXAM-STYLE QUESTION Q9 Explain how the Holocaust has challenged Jewish beliefs, and explain responses to the challenges posed by the Holocaust. (8 marks)

EXAM-STYLE QUESTION Q10 *"All suffering, including the Holocaust, is a test of faith."* Do you agree with this? Give reasons for your answer. Show that you have thought about other points of view. (4 marks)

Different Jewish Traditions

Q1 What does it mean for someone to be a "secular Jew"?

Q2 There are many different Jewish cultures and traditions.

a) Where do Sephardic Jews come from?
b) Where do Ashkenazi Jews come from?

Q3 In Judaism, there are two main types of commandment — ritual and moral.

a) Which type of commandment do Progressive Jews see as binding and unchangeable?
b) Which type of commandment do Progressive Jews think can be changed and adapted?

Q4 The Torah is interpreted differently by Orthodox and Progressive Jews.

a) What is the Orthodox Jewish opinion of how people should view the Torah today?
b) What is the Progressive Jewish opinion of how people should view the Torah today?

Q5 What ultra-Orthodox Jewish movement was started by a rabbi called the Baal Shem Tov?

Q6 Which Jewish tradition prays for the physical rebuilding of the Temple in Jerusalem?

a) Reform Judaism b) Orthodox Judaism c) Liberal Judaism

Q7 Name two traditions in which women can be rabbis.

Q8 Name one tradition that uses only Hebrew in synagogue services.

Q9 What does Liberal Judaism teach about personal choice in religion?

Q10 Describe the major differences between Orthodox Judaism and Reform Judaism. (8 marks)

EXAM-STYLE QUESTION Q11 *"The Torah is God's word. It's wrong to change or adapt it."* Do you agree with this? Give reasons for your answer. Show that you have thought about other points of view. (8 marks)

Judaism and Day-to-Day Life

Q1 How many commandments are there in the Torah?

Q2 What is the Hebrew word for commandment? What about more than one commandment?

Q3 There are different kinds of commandments in the Torah.

a) What is meant by a 'moral commandment'?
b) What is meant by a 'ritual commandment'?

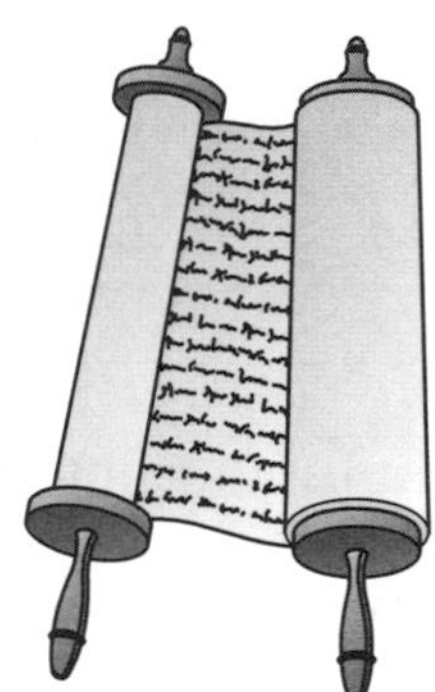

Q4 *Jews believe that the commandments and laws given by God are the main way that God communicates with humans.*

What do Jews believe is the best way of responding to God?

Q5 What two things do religious Jews believe that they should do in order to be considered good moral people?

Q6 When deciding what to do for the best, in what order do religious Jews consider the following Jewish teachings?

The Talmud

The Torah

Wider Jewish teaching (e.g. the *Mishneh Torah* commentaries of Maimonides).

Q7 Answer these questions about the mikveh.

a) What is a mikveh?
b) When do women go to the mikveh?
c) When do men go to the mikveh?

EXAM-STYLE QUESTION Q8 Describe a mikveh and its uses. (6 marks)

EXAM-STYLE QUESTION Q9 Explain how mitzvot are relevant to Jews in their everyday lives. (8 marks)

The Synagogue

Q1 Give two other words for "synagogue".

Q2 Which symbols might you see on the outside of a synagogue? Choose from:

Cross	Seven-branched candlestick
Shield	Crescent moon
Six-pointed star	Mickey Mouse

Q3 Match each of the four features of a synagogue below to the correct descriptions:

Aron Hakodesh	Raised platform with reading desk, normally in the centre of the hall.
Ner Tamid	Large cupboard or alcove, with doors or a screen, set on the wall facing Jerusalem. This is the most important item of furniture in a synagogue.
Sefer Torah	Parchment scrolls that must be handwritten by a sofer (scribe), and are usually decorated.
Bimah or Almemar	A light which never goes out. It represents the menorah which was always kept alight in the Temple.

Q4 *The rabbi's role is similar in some ways to that of a minister in a Christian church — he leads prayers, conducts weddings and funerals, etc.*

Explain why rabbis are not considered to be priests.

Q5 *Many synagogues have a 'chazan' as well as a rabbi.*

a) Give another name for a chazan.

b) Describe the role of a chazan.

EXAM-STYLE QUESTION Q6 a) Describe the main features of a synagogue. (4 marks)

b) Explain the reasons for these features. (4 marks)

EXAM-STYLE QUESTION Q7 *"The synagogue should be the centre of Jewish social life."* Do you agree with this? Give reasons for your answer and refer to Jewish beliefs. Make sure you show you've thought about another point of view. (8 marks)

Signs and Symbols

Q1 Why are there no pictures of God in synagogues, or in Jewish homes?

Q2 The mezuzah is an important Jewish symbol.

a) What is a mezuzah?
b) Where are mezuzot found?
c) What are mezuzot for?
d) What Bible passages are contained in a mezuzah?

Q3 Why do many Jewish men and boys wear a yarmulka?

Q4 Tefillin are an important part of Jewish ritual dress.

a) What are tefillin?
b) Where are tefillin worn?
c) When are tefillin worn?
d) What Bible passages are contained in the tefillin?
e) What do the tefillin remind the wearer to do?

Q5 *Some Jewish men wear a special shawl during prayers.*

a) What is this prayer shawl called?
b) What are the fringes on the prayer shawl called?

EXAM-STYLE QUESTION Q6 Describe ritual dress sometimes worn by Jewish men. (8 marks)

Q7 *"Being visibly different just makes people prejudiced against you."*
Do you agree with this? Refer to Judaism in your answer. Give reasons for your answer, and show that you have thought about other points of view. (7 marks)

In the Exam, they might give you some boxes Tefillin...

In the Exam, you can either be asked about a specific piece of ritual dress, or you can be asked to describe the whole lot. So there's only one thing for it... yep, learn everything about everything on this page.

Judaism and Children

Q1 The ceremony of circumcision is an important rite of passage in Judaism.

a) What is the Hebrew name for the ceremony of circumcision?

b) How old are Jewish baby boys when they are circumcised?

c) What is the Hebrew name for the man who carries out the circumcision?

Q2 How old are Jewish baby boys when they're ceremonially "bought back" from a life in the priesthood?

Q3 What is the Sephardic ceremony for naming a daughter called?

Q4 Give two examples of things that Jewish schools teach on top of the regular school curriculum.

Q5 *Some Jewish festivals have features that specifically involve children.* Give two examples of these features.

Q6 Judaism has different coming of age ceremonies for boys and girls.

a) At what age does a Jewish boy become Bar Mitzvah?

b) What can a boy wear once he is Bar Mitzvah?

c) What are the three parts of a Bar Mitzvah celebration?

d) What are Bat Mitzvah and Bat Chayil?

Q7 Describe the ceremony of Brit Milah. (5 marks)

Q8 Explain why Bar Mitzvah is so important to Jewish families and communities. (4 marks)

Jewish Beliefs about Death

Q1 According to the Torah, where do the souls of the dead go?

Q2 What do religious Jews believe will happen to the dead when the Messiah comes?

Q3 According to Jewish tradition, what should a dying person do just before they die?

Q4 Why do bereaved family members make a little rip in their clothes?

Q5 What is done with the dead body immediately after is it washed?

Q6 When they die, Jewish people are often buried in a shroud and coffin.

a) What kind of shroud are Jews buried in?

b) What kind of coffin are Jews buried in?

Q7 What happens at the funeral service in the synagogue?

Q8 What is the name of the prayer Jewish men recite for the dead?

Q9 Judaism has various customs designed to help comfort the bereaved.

a) What is the first week after the funeral called?

b) What four things must the bereaved family avoid doing in the week after the funeral?

c) What happens in the month after the funeral?

d) For how long must someone mourn after the death of a parent?

EXAM-STYLE QUESTION Q10 Describe Jewish rituals and customs related to death, funerals and mourning. (8 marks)

EXAM-STYLE QUESTION Q11 Explain how Jewish funeral and mourning rituals might help comfort the family of someone who has died. (7 marks)

There are loads of Jewish teachings about death...

This is quite a heavy page, so to lighten the mood slightly, why not learn a bit of Hebrew... "*Ani ohev otach.*" Which means "I love you," (so I'm told). Which makes for a lovely, warm and fluffy end to the page.

Jewish Prayer and the Sabbath

Q1 At what times of day are the three daily prayers?

Q2 What is the name for the minimum number of people required to have a service in the synagogue?

Q3 Why do Jews celebrate and rest on the Sabbath?

Q4 *The start and finish of Shabbat varies through the year.*

a) When does Shabbat begin?

b) When does Shabbat end?

Q5 *Friday evening services at the synagogue have singing.*

a) Who leads the singing?

b) Why is the singing not accompanied by musical instruments?

Q6 Describe the Saturday morning service at the synagogue.

Q7 Write down three things that Jewish families do to prepare for Shabbat at home.

Q8 Who lights the Shabbat candles?

Q9 What is the purifying ceremony at the start of Shabbat called?

Q10 Describe the havdalah ceremony at the end of Shabbat.

EXAM-STYLE QUESTION Q11 Explain why Sabbath observance is so important to religious Jews. and describe the synagogue services that take place over Shabbat. (7 marks)

EXAM-STYLE QUESTION Q12 *"Celebrating Shabbat at home is more important than celebrating at the synagogue."*
Do you agree with this? Give reasons for your answer, and show that you have thought about other points of view. (5 marks)

Pilgrimage, Food and Fasting

Q1 *In the days when the Temple was still standing in Jerusalem, Jews went to the Temple for three festivals.*

What were the names of these festivals?

Q2 *Three places are particularly important to Jewish pilgrims.*

a) Where is the Wailing Wall?
b) What happened at Masada?
c) What is the Hebrew name for the Holocaust Memorial?

Q3 What is the opposite of kosher?

Q4 For each of these foods, write down if they are kosher or not. If they aren't kosher, write down why not.

a) Beef b) Pork c) Lamb d) Cod e) Prawns f) Eel

Q5 What's the important rule about meat and dairy?

Q6 How must animals be slaughtered to be considered kosher?

Q7 What does fasting symbolise in Judaism?

Q8 What is Rosh Hashanah?

Q9 On Rosh Hashanah, a *shofar* is blown — what does this symbolise?

Q10 Rosh Hashanah and Yom Kippur are known as the *Days of Awe*.

a) What is Yom Kippur?
b) What comes between Rosh Hashanah and Yom Kippur?
c) For how long must Jews fast on Yom Kippur?

EXAM-STYLE QUESTION Q11 Explain Jewish beliefs concerning the significance of the Days of Awe. (8 marks)

EXAM-STYLE QUESTION Q12 Explain what is meant by the Kashrut, and the implications of Kashrut for a Jew's everyday life. (7 marks)

Jewish Festivals

Q1 *The Jewish festival of Purim is also known as Lots.*

a) When is Purim?

b) Whose story does it commemorate?

Q2 What does Shavuot commemorate?

Q3 *In early autumn, Jewish families camp out in shelters they build themselves.*

a) What is the name of this festival?

b) What is one of these shelters called?

c) What does this festival commemorate?

Q4 Describe the events commemorated by Pesach.

Q5 *Before Pesach, Jewish households get rid of all ordinary bread (even the crumbs), all yeast and baking powder and some kinds of flour.*

Why do they do this?

Q6 Give five components of the Seder meal.

Q7 Which festival celebrates the end of one round of Torah readings and the start of the next one?

Q8 Write down at which festival each of these things happens:

a) Children play with spinning tops and doughnuts are eaten.

b) People wear fancy dress costumes.

c) Cheesecake is eaten.

d) Men dance seven times around the synagogue.

Q9 a) Describe the Passover meal. (4 marks)

b) Explain the importance of Pesach to Jews. (3 marks)

EXAM-STYLE QUESTION Q10 Give an outline of the celebration of Sukkot. (6 marks)

A nice cheerful page to finish with...

This is a nice page to finish the section with — with its doughnuts and spinning tops and fancy dress costumes. But even though the subject matter's a bit more cheery, it still needs learning.

Basic Islamic Beliefs

Q1 What is tawhid?

Q2 What is shirk?

Q3 What is the Arabic name for the Muslim declaration of faith?

Q4 *The first part of the Muslim declaration of faith is, "There is no God but Allah."*

What is the second part of the declaration of faith?

Q5 How many times a day must Muslims pray?

Q6 *Muslims wash before prayers.*

a) Name three parts of the body that a Muslim must wash before praying.

b) What is the Arabic word for washing before prayers?

Q7 What is Zakah?

Q8 What is Sawm?

Q9 *The Fifth Pillar of Islam is Hajj — a pilgrimage.*

a) Where do Muslims go on pilgrimage?

b) What's special about the clothes Muslims wear on pilgrimage?

Q10 Briefly describe Muslim beliefs about Allah, and explain why Shirk is the very worst sin in Islam. (6 marks)

EXAM-STYLE QUESTION Q11 What are the five pillars of Islam? (5 marks)

Work, don't shirk...

There's more on Muslim beliefs about Allah on p7 and p9 of the CGP Revision Guide. Learn the Arabic names of the five pillars of Islam, as well as the English versions. The Exam paper will probably use the Arabic names.

Prophets and Angels

Q1 *According to Islam, Allah is so great that he doesn't communicate with humans directly — he uses prophets and messengers to carry his messages.*

a) What is the Arabic word for the idea of having prophets and messengers?

b) What is the Arabic word for prophet?

Q2 Which of the following statements best describes the way that Allah communicates with humankind?

a) *"Allah gives his message direct to a prophet, who passes it on to everyone else."*

b) *"Allah speaks directly to everyone."*

c) *"Allah gives his message to angels. Angels pass on Allah's word to prophets, and the prophets pass it on to everyone else."*

Q3 Give three ways in which angels are different from human beings, according to Islam.

Q4 How many prophets are named in the Qur'an?

Q5 *There are five Mighty Prophets, according to Islam.*

a) Who are the five Mighty Prophets?

b) Who was the first prophet?

c) Which prophet was asked by Allah to sacrifice his own son, as a test of faith?

d) Which prophet was given the tablets of the law?

Q6 Do Muslims believe that Allah gave humans free will to choose their own actions?

Q7 What's the Arabic name for the idea of taking responsibility for the world on God's behalf?

EXAM-STYLE QUESTION Q8 Explain Muslim teachings about khalifah. (8 marks)

EXAM-STYLE QUESTION Q9 Describe Muslim beliefs about risalah. (8 marks)

The Qur'an

Q1 Do Muslims view the Qur'an as the literal word of God?

Q2 How did Muhammad and his followers make sure that none of the revelations of the Qur'an were forgotten or lost?

Q3 Who made sure that there was only one authoritative and 100% correct version of the Qur'an?

Q4 Why is it not really OK to read the Qur'an translated into English?

Q5 Describe three ways that many Muslims show special respect to the Qur'an.

Q6 During which month of the Islamic year is the Qur'an read from beginning to end during services at the mosque?

Q7 The Qur'an is divided up into various parts.

a) What is a surah?

b) What is an ayat?

Q8 What is the bismillah? Where in the Qur'an would you find the bismillah?

Q9 *There are other important Islamic texts as well as the Qur'an.*

a) What are the collected sayings of Muhammad called?

b) What is the biography of Muhammad's actions and way of life called?

EXAM-STYLE QUESTION Q10 Explain how the Qur'an and the Hadith affect the daily lives of ordinary modern Muslims. (7 marks)

EXAM-STYLE QUESTION Q11 Describe Muslim beliefs about the Qur'an. (8 marks)

EXAM-STYLE QUESTION Q12 *"People need a holy book to tell them how to behave."*
Do you agree with this? Give reasons for your answer and show you've thought about another point of view. Refer to Islam in your answer. (5 marks)

The Prophet Muhammad

Q1 When and where was Muhammad born?

Q2 How did Muhammad meet and get to know his first wife, Khadijah?

Q3 Where was Muhammad when Allah sent the angel Jibrail to him?

Q4 Which of the following were parts of the message that Jibrail told Muhammad to pass on to the people of Makkah?

a) Be honest in business, and look after the poor in society.
b) Take only one wife.
c) Worship only one God, Allah.
d) Prepare for a great flood.
e) Listen to the words of Muhammad, prophet of Allah.
f) Do God's will, or you'll end up in Hell.

Q5 Describe how the people of Makkah reacted to Muhammad's preaching.

Q6 Where did Muhammad go in 622?

Q7 What is the Hijrah, and why was it a big turning point for Muhammad?

Q8 *Makkah and Madinah went to war.*

a) What happened at the battle of Badr?
b) What happened at the battle of Uhud?
c) When did Muhammad and the Muslims of Madinah take over Makkah?

EXAM-STYLE QUESTION Q9 Describe how God called Muhammad to be his Prophet. (8 marks)

EXAM-STYLE QUESTION Q10 Give an account of what Muhammad achieved after the Hijrah. (6 marks)

You say Mecca, and I say Makkah...

There are some things you just can't afford to go into the Exam hall not knowing. And yep, when it comes to Islam, Muhammad and the Qur'an are two such topics. So buckle down and get the stuff learnt.

Different Islamic Traditions

Q1 What are the two main strands of Islam?

Q2 What were the names of the first four Caliphs?

Q3 Which group accepted the appointment of the fifth Caliph?

Q4 What do Sunnis call the first four Caliphs?

Q5 According to Sunnis, does Allah give anyone after Muhammad special revelation?

Q6 Which Muslim tradition believes that imams are just prayer leaders in the mosque?

Q7 What do Shi'ites call the leaders of Islam who are given special knowledge by Allah?

Q8 *Muslims read the sayings of Muhammad for moral guidance.*

Whose sayings do Shi'ite Muslims also read for moral guidance?

Q9 Whose martyrdom do Shi'ite Muslims commemorate?

Q10 What are ayatollahs?

EXAM-STYLE QUESTION Q11 Explain the differences between the Sunni idea of religious leaders and the Shi'a idea of religious leaders. (8 marks)

EXAM-STYLE QUESTION Q12 *"Muslims should all agree about religion"*
Do you agree with this? Give reasons for your answer, showing that you've thought about another point of view. (5 marks)

Ta-caliph out of my book and learn this...

Luckily, you don't need to know the finest details of the history and customs of both traditions, just the basics. The big difference between the two main traditions of Islam is their idea of religious leadership.

Sufism

Q1 What are the aims of Sufism?

"It is not enough to observe the rituals of Islam... A humble soul may be religious even though ignorant of interpretations of the Qur'an. The core of religion is to repent of one's sins, purge the heart of all but God."

Q2 What do Sufis try and do to help them search for the mystical meaning of the Qur'an?

Q3 Which of the following are parts of the Sufi way of life?

a) Sacred poetry and chanting	d) Meditation
b) Worship of Muhammad	e) Self-denial
c) Trying to live like Muhammad	f) Visits to the beach

Q4 *Most Muslims believe that obeying the rules of Islam is the heart of Islam.*

What do Sufis believe is the heart of Islam?

Q5 Who are the Whirling Dervishes, and why do they whirl?

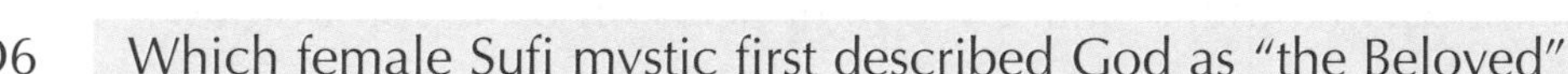

Q6 Which female Sufi mystic first described God as "the Beloved"?

Q7 Why do some Muslims disapprove of the Sufi idea of merging with God?

EXAM-STYLE QUESTION Q8 Describe the differences between the Sufi tradition and mainstream Islam. (6 marks)

EXAM-STYLE QUESTION Q9 Explain how Sufis try to discover hidden mystical truths and become at one with God. (8 marks)

EXAM-STYLE QUESTION Q10 *"Sufism is a deviation from the right path of Islam"*
Do you agree with this? Give reasons for your answer, showing that you've thought about another point of view. (5 marks)

Islam and the Shari'ah

Q1 How do Muslims please Allah?

Q2 What happens to Muslims who have failed to please Allah?

Q3 What is the literal meaning of the word Islam?

Q4 What is shari'ah?

Q5 *Shari'ah comes from several sources.*
What are the three most important sources of shari'ah?

Q6 If Muslim scholars can't find the solution to a new problem by looking in the old books and traditions, what do they do?

Q7 How do scholars and lawyers trust that they'll make the right decision on a point of law?

Q8 Describe a situation where analogy is used to make a judgement on a moral question.

An analogy is when you find a similar situation and apply a rule for that situation to the original one too.

Q9 Explain how Islamic scholars and lawyers might decide whether something is right or wrong according to shari'ah. (10 marks)

Q10 *"People can only be good Muslims if they read the Islamic holy books."*
Do you agree with this? Give reasons for your answer, showing that you've thought about another point of view. (5 marks)

The Shari-ah is a kind of rule book for Muslim life...

While on the subject of words for groups of things (ahem)... it's a little known fact that a group of ferrets is called a 'business', a number of rooks goes by the name of a 'parliament', and several elk gathered together are known as a 'gang'. And what's a 'drunkship'... that's right, a load of cobblers. All true.

Islamic Living and Jihad

Q1 The Shari'ah says that things are either halal or haram.

a) What does halal mean?
b) What does haram mean?

Q2 What dress rule applies to both Muslim men and Muslim women?

Q3 What is a hijab?

Q4 How must animals be killed in order to be halal?

Q5 Which of the following fats are okay to cook with?

a) Vegetable oil b) Beef dripping c) Bacon fat

Q6 *Muslims must not harm others.*
Explain why this means that Muslims must not gamble.

Q7 Why are loans and mortgages from Western banks forbidden to Muslims?

Q8 What is the greater Jihad?

Q9 *War to defend Islam against its enemies is part of the lesser Jihad.*
What else is part of the lesser Jihad?

EXAM-STYLE QUESTION Q10 Describe what the Qur'an says about suitable clothes for Muslims. (6 marks)

EXAM-STYLE QUESTION Q11 Explain why Muslims might have problems dealing with investment and finance in a non-Muslim country. (6 marks)

EXAM-STYLE QUESTION Q12 *"You can't expect Muslims to follow the rules on halal food in a non-Muslim country."*
Do you agree with this? Give reasons for your answer, showing that you've thought about another point of view. (5 marks)

The Mosque

Q1 Give another word for mosque.

Q2 *Mosques have at least one dome and one minaret.*

a) Why do mosques have a dome?

b) Why do mosques have a minaret?

Q3 What job does a muezzin do?

Q4 What is the purpose of a mihrab?

Q5 What is a minbar?

Q6 What is the name of the person who leads prayers in the mosque?

Q7 Are women allowed to lead prayers? Choose the right answer from the options below.

a) *Women are never allowed to lead prayers.*

b) *Women can lead all prayers in the mosque.*

c) *Women can only lead other women and children in prayer.*

Q8 Why is the mosque decorated with calligraphy instead of pictures of Muhammad?

Q9 Give two examples of things that Muslims learn at the Madrassah.

Q10 In which tradition of Islam are imams considered holy men?

EXAM-STYLE QUESTION Q11 a) Describe the main features of a mosque. (4 marks)

b) What are the reasons for these features? (8 marks)

EXAM-STYLE QUESTION Q12 *"Muslims can pray anywhere they like, so mosques aren't necessary to Muslim life."*
Do you agree with this? Give reasons for your answer, showing that you've thought about another point of view. (5 marks)

Worship and Prayer

Q1 What is the first pillar of Islam?

Q2 Why do Muslims wash before prayers?

Q3 What is qiblah and why is it important?

Q4 What's the special name for Friday prayers in the mosque?

Q5 Why can daily prayer be difficult for Muslims living and working in non-Muslim countries?

Q6 Between which two times of day must Muslims fast during Ramadan?

Q7 As well as food, which of the following are forbidden during fasting hours in Ramadan?

a) *Drinking water*
b) *Drinking milk*
c) *Having sex*
d) *Smoking*
e) *Brushing the teeth with toothpaste*

Q8 Who can be excused from fasting during Ramadan?

Q9 Write down two things that Muslims believe fasting is for.

Q10 What is the name of the big festival that celebrates the end of Ramadan?

Q11 Whose story is commemorated by the repeated journeys between Safa and Marwa?

EXAM-STYLE QUESTION Q12 Describe the rituals surrounding salah. (6 marks)

EXAM-STYLE QUESTION Q13 Describe and explain what Muslims do on the Hajj. (12 marks)

What does the Imam sleep on — the five pillows of Islam...

If you've been praying for the end of the book then good news, it's only a couple of pages away. Only a few more questions on the Five Pillars of Islam, Birth and Death to go.

Birth and Death Ceremonies

Q1 According to Islam, what should be the first word a baby hears?

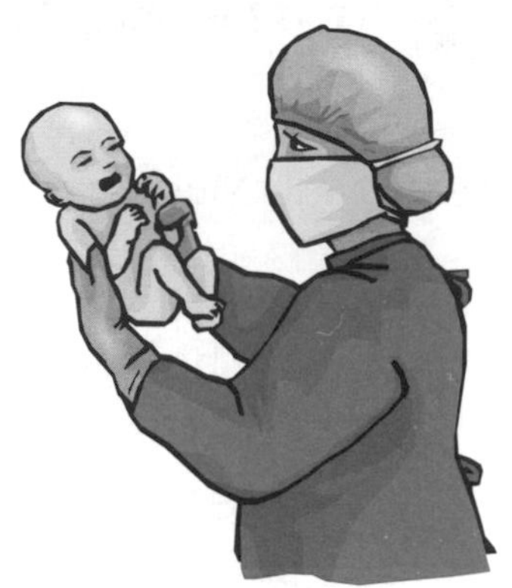

Q2 How old is a baby when it's named?

Q3 What is the Muslim naming ceremony called?

Q4 *Parents donate some gold or silver to charity when the baby is named.*
How do they work out how much gold or silver to give?

Q5 Is circumcision required for Muslim boys?

Q6 What three things should friends and relatives do to help a dying Muslim?

Q7 How is the body of a Muslim prepared for the funeral?

Q8 *After someone's death, their body must be laid to rest in a certain way.*

a) Which side are the dead lying on when they're buried — right or left?
b) Where must the dead person's face be pointing?

Q9 How long is the "official" religious mourning period?

EXAM-STYLE QUESTION Q10 Describe a Muslim funeral. (6 marks)

EXAM-STYLE QUESTION Q11 Describe the ceremony of aqiqa. (8 marks)

So that's the end of the book, then...

The final page of the final section is over... so you can relax, take a deep breath and have a nice cup of tea. Then just make sure you can answer any question in the whole book, and you can go do your Exam.